Foreword by NORM

author of *Awakening Osiris*

ANCIENT EGYPTIAN MAGIC

ELEANOR HARRIS

WEISER BOOKS

This edition first published in 2015 by Weiser Books
an imprint of Red Wheel/Weiser, LLC
With offices at:
65 Parker Street, Suite 7
Newburyport, MA 01950
www.redwheelweiser.com
Sign up for our newsletter and special offers by going to
www.redwheelweiser.com/newsletter.

 Originally published in 1998 as *Ancient Egyptian Divination and Magic* by Samuel Weiser, Inc., ISBN: 1-57863-036-3.

ISBN: 978-1-57863-591-7
Library of Congress Cataloging-in-Publication Data available upon request

Cover design by Jim Warner
Typeset in Palatino Linotype and Times New Roman

Printed in the United States of America
MG
10 9 8 7 6 5 4 3 2 1

This book was written with love for my father, Charles R. Lillie. *Wón-j n mr(w)t-k* ("I shine through love of you").

I dedicate this book also to my husband, Philip A. Harris, who knows the solar Eye of Ra. Together, we shall love eternally.

Special thanks to the loyal scholar-magicians of the House of Life, who have helped make this book possible.

Contents

List of Figures

Foreword

Perhaps you came to this book wanting to learn something about how to make magic—and you will. The most important thing Eleanor Harris will teach you, however, is how to make relationship, because ultimately that is what all magic-making is about. You will learn words of power and what makes the magic soar, which is aligning oneself to the creative source, willingness, discrimination, and an understanding of the natural laws of karma, thought, and vibration, among others. Eleanor Harris sets us off on the right foot by introducing us to the many ways in which to make, develop and maintain an active (rather than passive) relationship with the many manifestations of the divine as the gods and goddesses of the ancient Egyptians.

One reason magic works is through the focus of the mind. As metaphysicians one must develop both focused intention on that which we will manifest, but also attention, which is the receptive opening of consciousness that operates through true communication with the numinous. As with any relationship, the more you put into it the more you get out of it.

The magical, meditative recipes Harris details derived from ancient manuscripts show the novice in the mysteries how to increase focus through magical means and practice. Well-researched and spiced with entertaining stories of magical doings, this book brims over with her insights, some little-known (by me, anyway) facts and practical applications.

Her chapter on words of power underscores the maxim behind all magic: Thoughts (and words) are things. "Words are a map of the will," Harris says, "and ceremony is the emphasis." Her analysis of symbol and of trance states in divination offers a comprehensive understanding of psychic or altered states and how the brain accesses intuitive information. Then her practical ideas lead you there into the realm of evocative communication with the spiritual world.

I happily recommend this book and its author to all who seek an understanding of how and why the ancient Egyptian magical path is still relevant to practical metaphysicians in the 21st century.

—Normandi Ellis
Author of
Awakening Osiris and
Imagining the World into Existence

Introduction

First and foremost, this is a practical manual and study of the native divination and magical practices of ancient Egypt. All of the instruction and material herein is authentic, as derived from ancient Egyptian magical papyri. *The Leyden Papyrus,* an Egyptian magical papyrus, and *The Papyrus Ani,* the *Egyptian Book of the Dead,* and many more renowned literary works have contributed to this book.

The aim of this book is to provide you, the contemporary student, with a practical collection of Egyptian divination and magical instruction. The teachings and rituals of Egyptian magic are as alive today as they were in predynastic and prehistoric Egypt. Like hidden treasure, the wisdom and practice awaits your discovery.

Written for the beginner, yet enticing to more experienced practitioners, this guide celebrates the world-renowned mystery, tradition, and ceremonial prestige of Egyptian magic.

Within this user-friendly text, you will be led step-by-step through religious and magical philosophy, techniques, instruction, and divination and magical formulas thousands of years old. You will:

- Explore the Egyptian religious and magical philosophies that are suitable for your own spiritual and magical quest today;
- Discover how the Egyptians developed their magical practices and why they were successful;
- Find out how the ancient temples and priesthoods functioned, and how you can create your own working environment today;
- Create and wear ancient priesthood clothing, and

learn how to make and use the ritual tools of Egyptian magicians;

- Examine the use of amulets, figures, pictures, written magic, spells, words of power, and more magical items and techniques to empower your magic;
- Come to understand the format and purpose of Egyptian magical ceremony and how to design your own;
- Learn how to fire, water, and oil scry, have dream visions, shape-shift into a god-form, sound the secret names of the deities to acquire their awesome power, conjure dead spirits, make and use ancient eye-paint to see invoked deities, understand and write your own Egyptian magical formulas, make and use amulets, work defensive magic; cast love, protection, and healing spells; evoke spirits into statues and other magical objects, use sex magic, bring good fortune, and more exciting acts of sorcery;
- Revive the wisdom of the ancient Egyptians through work with dreams, prognostications, transformations, and more.

The instructions herein include original formulas of divination and magic that you can use immediately. This alleviates your tedious research to compile working data from ancient magical papyri and other historical literature. Everything you need to know is here at your fingertips.

With this book as your guide, you can learn to use the ancient and potent magical arts that captured the fascination of ancient Hebrew, Greek, and Roman writers, all of whom considered the Egyptians experts in the occult sciences.

Chapter One

Understanding Egyptian Religious and Magical Philosophy

Ignorance is Darkness —Egyptian proverb

From the earliest times, magic was developed largely by the Egyptians in relation both to the dead and the living.[1] The belief in magic is older in Egypt than the belief in God.[2] Egyptian religion was grounded in a firm and active belief in the importance of magic. Ancient Egyptians believed in, and aspired to use, the power of magical amulets, spells, scripts, names, and intricate ceremonies. To best understand Egyptian magic, you need to understand their religious and magical philosophy.

Religious Philosophy

The Egyptians did not maintain a universal system of religious belief. Dogma did not exist. There were no holy texts

[1] F. L. Griffith and Herbert Thompson, eds., *The Leyden Papyrus: An Egyptian Magical Book* (New York: Dover, 1974), p. 6.

[2] E. A. Wallis Budge, *Egyptian Magic* (New York: Dover, 1971), p. ix.

defining strict religious doctrines requiring conformity. In polytheism, there was tolerance. The ancient Egyptians were peaceful, kind, and very aware of family values. Their religious dealings reflected this in that there were no persecutions in the name of religion.

Egyptians revered and respected all of natural existence. They did not attempt to persuade or force non-Egyptians to worship their deities, nor did they degrade the beliefs of others. In fact, the Egyptians were open-minded and receptive to other cultures' belief systems.

Ancient Egyptian religion is puzzling to a degree; it resembles Judaism, Islam, and Christianity in that it propounded a belief in a central god, the Creator, but it was also polytheistic.

Whether polytheism grew from monotheism in Egypt, or monotheism from polytheism, will remain a mystery. The evidence of the pyramid texts shows that, already in the 5th Dynasty, monotheism and polytheism flourished side by side.[3]

While the ancient Egyptians had a pantheon of gods and goddesses, they believed in one central god who was the Creator, invisible and eternal. This one god created all in existence. This god was divine, but had lived upon the Earth and had suffered a cruel death at the hands of his enemies. He had risen from the dead and had become the God and Pharaoh of the world beyond the grave.[4] This god was Ausar.

The following outline of beliefs taken from native religious works, some calculated to be between six and seven thousand years old, describes the basic composition of Egyptian religious philosophy:

---

[3] E. A. Wallis Budge, *Egyptian Book of the Dead* (New York: Dover. 1967), p. xciii.

[4] E. A. Wallis Budge, *Egyptian Book of the Dead,* p. xiii.

- A central god, the Creator;
- A company of gods and goddesses possessing human-like emotion and human-animal characteristics;
- Divine truth, order, and judgment;
- Divine battle between Order and Chaos;
- Resurrection;
- Immortality.

From primitive times and well into more civilized periods, Egyptian religious beliefs remained much the same. The Egyptians were immaculate record keepers and very conservative in maintaining early traditions. New insights gained with the passage of time were merely added to the main body of beliefs.

Order and Chaos at War

The Egyptians believed the forces of primal chaos posed a continuous threat to the world. The creation of the world had occurred in conjunction with the creation of social order and kingship, and the harmony of the universe could be preserved by practicing the principal of *maat*,·divine truth, justice, and order. The principal of maat was the basis of the Egyptian religion, and was symbolized by the goddess Maat. She reigned over the equilibrium of the universe, the divine order of all things, and the regular cycles of the Sun, the Moon, the stars, the seasons, and time itself. Although it was clear these chaotic forces had been tamed, only the deities could protect and defeat the eternally present threat of chaos.

The Nine Bodies: A Religious Theory

Egyptians believed that humans and other living creatures consisted of nine "bodies." These nine bodies define why the Egyptians believed that it was possible to invoke a creature's life force into a statue, and thereby gain the creature's power. They believed in ghosts and apparitions, which were made possible by the existence of the "ka" body; and the "khu" body, discussed below. Through different bodies, the Egyptians communicated with the dead, projected out-of-body, assumed other creatures' power, and enjoyed other abilities that you can share today.

The nine bodies are defined and discussed below. By learning the principles of each, you will understand their uses in magic that are described in later chapters.

Khat, the natural body: which is translated as something which is able to decay. It is the physical body. The word also applies to the mummified body in a tomb. Funeral ceremonies on the day of burial have the power to transform the khat into the spiritual body, the "sāḥu." The physical body was given to the Earth upon death but the soul resided in heaven. This proves Egyptians believed in an afterlife, eternal life, and resurrection.

Sāḥu, the spiritual body: describes a physical body that has obtained a degree of knowledge, power, and glory. It evolves thereby into the sāḥu, which is everlasting and incorruptible. The sāḥu has the ability to become related to the soul and to communicate with it. When the physical body changes into the sāḥu body, it ascends into the heavens to dwell with the gods and the righteous.

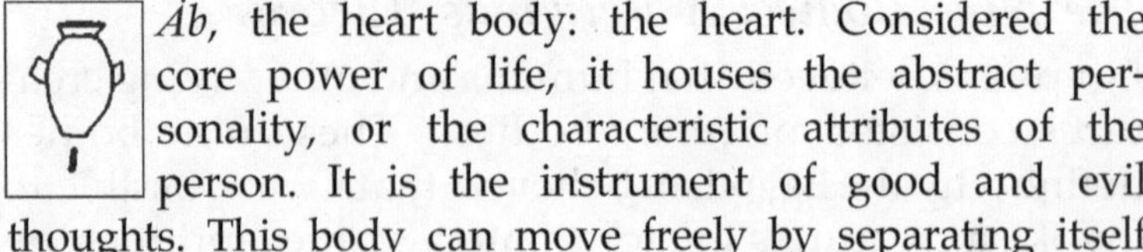

Ȧb, the heart body: the heart. Considered the core power of life, it houses the abstract personality, or the characteristic attributes of the person. It is the instrument of good and evil thoughts. This body can move freely by separating itself from, or uniting with, the physical body at will. It also enjoys life with the gods in heaven.[5]

Ka, the double body: literally describes a "double" of image and genius. Considered a copy of the physical body, (compare to contemporary "astral body"), the ka was offered meat, wine, and other delicacies at funeral ceremonies to sustain it after physical death. The ka dwelt within the deceased's statue, just as the ka of a deity dwells within its statue. Someone who wished to communicate with the deceased read a message, left a written message on papyrus in the tomb, or tied a statue of the deceased in the tomb. Since the ka lived therein, it could, of course, observe and understand.[6]

There was a priesthood in Egypt, termed *Priests of Ka,* who performed services, worshiped, and left offerings for the ka in a special chamber within the tomb, called the "ka chapel." After physical death, the ka required offerings of food and drink. If food and drink were scarce, the ka was given offerings painted upon the walls of the tomb. Magical intent transformed the pictures into suitable nourishment.

Ba, the soul body: means something roughly equivalent to "sublime," or "noble." The ba dwells in the ka. It continues to possess both substance and form after death. It is depicted in hieroglyphs as a human-headed hawk and its nature is ethereal. The ba can revisit the body in the tomb, re-animate it, and converse with it. It can take any shape desired and passes into heaven to dwell eternally with other perfect souls. Like the ka, the ba needs

---

5 E. A. Wallis Budge, *Egyptian Book of the Dead,* p. lxi, kii.

6 Leemans, *Monuments Egyptiens,* Partie II, pp. 11, 183, 184 referred to in *Egyptian Magic,* p. 219.

food and drink to sustain itself. It also partook of funeral offerings.

Khaibit, the shadow body: is the shadow of the human that connects with the ka and ba as they ingest funeral offerings and visit the tomb at will. The khaibit is associated to the soul, because it is believed to always be near it. The Egyptians considered it part of the human economy. It has an independent existence and is able to separate from the body to move as it pleases.

Khu, the spirit body: means translucent or shining and indicates the intangible casing of the body. It can be compared to the aura. The khu represents the intelligence, but in many hieroglyphic texts, it is spoken of as what we understand to be the spirit, which is why experts term it "the spirit body." The khus of the gods reside in heaven. Human khus, during funeral ceremonies, are surrounded by the khus of the gods and assisted to heaven. The khu is imperishable. A special magical formula prepared by the ancient priests enabled the khu of the deceased to pass from the tomb and into the realm of the gods.

The collected bodies of a man or woman, once in heaven, were attributed to Ausar. Like Ausar, the deceased had walked among the living ones and then, at death, resurrected to become a son/daughter of the Creator. The Egyptians believed in deification of the spiritual body.

Sekhem, the form body: represents the form of power of a man or woman. The word has been associated with the soul and the khu. At death, the sekhem is called to come among the khus in heaven.

The Egyptian Sun god, Ra, was often referred to as "sekhem ur," which means Great Sekhem or Great Power. In many contemporary Egyptian practices, the sekhem is considered very much a part of human life. It represents the power of the individual that can be built up and directed in magic.

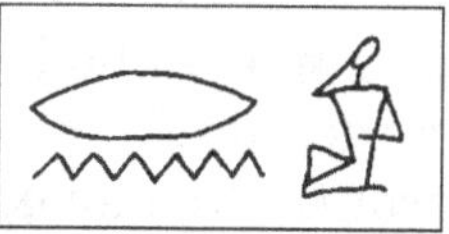

Ren, the name body: though rarely mentioned in books, describes the name by which the deceased was called in heaven. Egyptians believed that great power resided in words and names. They believed the gods knew the name of the deceased. The name of a person, deity, or creature was considered sacred and never-changing.

Humans and other creatures thus consisted of a physical body, a spiritual body, a heart, a double, a soul, a shadow, an intelligence/intangible ethereal casing, a form, and a name. All of these bodies were bound together, and the welfare of one concerned the welfare of all.

In contemporary circles, it is debated whether the ab, ka, or khaibit equates to the astral body. The Egyptians practiced shape-shifting, which is similar to astral projection. In certain texts, the ka is mentioned. In others, a particular body is not named. In chapter 4, you will learn how to shape-shift using the ka/double body.

Early Formation of Gods

Early Egyptians believed inanimate objects were endowed with magical and mystical power. Fossil belemnites, arrows, and a scepter were among the many objects recognized. Stones, such as red jasper, were regarded as sacred. Wood was sacred in Egypt, because trees were scarce. Egyptian traders are thought to have traded gold for wood to be used in the manufacture of their ritual tools and as the core of their statues.

Egyptians of the prehistoric era eventually began to give human form to their sacred animals and objects,[7] perhaps because inanimate or animal deities cannot converse easily with humans. A closer relationship was possible if the gods developed more human characteristics. Many gods and goddesses were equipped with a human body, but kept an animal head or other animal features. Later still, the deities were given full human form, but remained associated with, and at times were portrayed as, the original animal of their divinity.

The Creation of Animal Gods

Egyptians did not worship animals as animals; animals were thought to be incarnations of particular gods or goddesses. The animal was considered as the deity's manifestation upon Earth. This was no different than their belief that the Pharaoh was a visible incarnation of Ra, the Sun god.

Animal gods were localized. One province might worship a cat deity and another a bull god. An animal was chosen, it is believed, for special powers it possessed, or because of the fear that it caused. Although these characteristics played an important part, it may also have been a factor whether the animal was rare or abundant in a given area. Egyptologists are uncertain exactly why each animal god or goddess was chosen.

The practice of animism gave way to magical and mystical ideas about the objects and animals admired and revered. It was thought that their magical and powerful qualities could be invoked, absorbed by the magician-priest, and worked to obtain desires through magical formulas. It was believed that magicians

---

7 Barbara Watterson, *Gods of Ancient Egypt* (New York: Facts on File, 1985), p. 33.

could shape-shift into the chosen object, animal, or deity, could literally be transformed in mind, body, and soul in order to achieve magical goals. (You will learn how to shape-shift in chapter 4).

A Hierarchy of Gods

We can organize Egyptian deities into three categories:

Universal gods: cosmic deities who, as the central figures in Egyptian myths, were worshiped by cult temples. The Sun, Moon, storm, wind, and so on, were represented by gods and goddesses who became divine beings of intellectual understanding and worship. Cosmic gods were not fully developed until the Historic Era (post-3000 B.C.), when the Sun in particular became a universal god, worshiped throughout the land. Around 2500 B.C., the Sun god was elevated to the position of state god.[8]

Local gods: living creatures, associated with particular towns that were the earliest of Egyptian deities. Personal gods. Each town had its own local god.

Personal gods: objects or creatures that an individual believed sacred. Personal gods were very important to the average Egyptian, who was not allowed entrance into a temple. Much like the solitary pagan practitioners of today, these individuals were very content with worshiping through personal beliefs, working personal magic, and constructing their own shrines.

The Egyptians created and revered numerous deities by what they saw as beautiful and sacred qualities in the animals and environment. Every animal was considered a divine manifestation and were created into human-animal deities that each had a devoted following.

The creation of numerous deities is really not so peculiar. If you asked an Egyptian if he or she had seen

---

8 Barbara Watterson, *Gods of Ancient Egypt*, p. 33.

their cat-goddess Bast, they would say yes, for they witnessed a cat in their daily lives and in their temples. Not many religions have followers that can claim to actually see a manifestation of their deities, much less maintain such a closeness with them.

Several gods and goddess were revered simultaneously, and the individual was free to worship whichever he/she preferred.

Countless books exist detailing the gods and goddesses of ancient Egypt. Due to the fact that there are an estimated thousand or more, we will refrain from an in-depth examination of them here. The gods and goddesses discussed throughout this book are defined in the Glossary of Egyptian Gods and Goddesses, and within each chapter.

Magical Philosophy

Egyptian magic dates from the time when the predynastic and prehistoric dwellers in Egypt believed that the Earth, the underworld, the air, and the sky were peopled with countless beings, visible and invisible, that were potentially friendly or unfriendly to man, according to the operations of nature which they directed.[9] Primitive Egyptians believed these beings had attributes and personalities similar to their own: human emotions, desires, and weaknesses. These gods and goddesses, for which Egyptian religion is best known, provided the foundation for Egyptian magic, whose objective was to provide humankind control and dominance over these beings for the purpose of assuming their powers to carry out tasks and desires through magic.

Friendly beings were coaxed to assist the magician with offerings and attractive gifts. Unfriendly beings were flattered, pleaded with, or influenced by amulets, figures,

---

[9] E. A. Wallis Budge, *Egyptian Magic,* p. viii.

pictures, or secret names. Magical formulas were also designed and used. All of these tactics resulted in skilled mortals having access to beings who were more powerful than any enemy who threatened harm.

Just as Egyptians believed the world itself came into existence by the utterance of a single word, they believed that inanimate nature could be commanded by words of power. Gods, spirits, devils, weather-nothing could resist the power of words. Nature recognized the trained mind's strength. The elements, disease, and death were all susceptible to influence for positive or negative intent.

Early nations of Egypt practiced magic that caused the transfer of power from a being of the spirit world and worlds beyond to a man or woman knowledgeable in the magical arts. The theory was that the trained mind obtained great power to cause changes and achieve magical aims that were otherwise impossible. Ancient magicians could be endowed with both friendly and hostile powers, and with the power of the gods to control and direct as desired.

Religious ceremonies of later years are thought to have consisted of original magical and superstitious traditions. The religious books of ancient Egypt taught that magicians, and later priests, who were knowledgeable and skilled in magic had unlimited power to influence or cause change. The trained magician could recite and properly pronounce names and words of power that restored life to the dead, healed the sick, banished evil spirits, enabled human beings to shape-shift at will, and allowed doubles (astral bodies) to be projected into creatures or inanimate objects. By command, inanimate figures, objects, and pictures came to life and performed those tasks the magician desired. The use of poppets and figures that model human beings in the magical work of modem times is directly descended from Egyptian tradition.

Egyptians worked magic to influence every event in their lives, no matter how trivial or great. In the books of the "double house of life," the future was as well known as the past, and neither time nor distance could limit the operations of the magician's power.[10] The secrets of fate and destiny were revealed to, and could be controlled by, the skilled practitioner.

Even peasants held and practiced magical beliefs. Although the educated magician-priests practiced a more complex form of magic and added new techniques learned from foreigners. The peasants, not allowed entry into the temple or access to literature, practiced folk magic based upon superstition and old traditions.

Magical Misconceptions

Travelers from other lands who visited ancient Egypt recorded confused, contradicting reports of Egyptian magic that created misconceptions. There are two sources of the misconception that the Egyptians practiced black magic:

1. The ancient name of *Kamt* or *Qemt*, by which Egypt was known, means "dusky" or "black." It is one of the oldest names of Egypt, one that often was attributed to explanations of Egyptian religion and magic. The name describes the muddy land on each side of the Nile, which was of a dark color.
2. At an early period, the Egyptians were renowned for their aptitude in the working of metals. Early Greek writers tell us that Egyptians worked metals in an attempt to transmute them. These accounts state that quicksilver was used to separate silver and gold from native ore. From this process, a black residue resulted that was thought to contain individual characteristics of various metals and possess awesome powers. This substance was attributed to the god, Ausar's, body in the underworld; both were considered sources of life

[10] E. A. Wallis Budge, *Egyptian Magic*, p. xi.

force and power. The use of the black powder in magical spells was called "black magic" by scholars of the time.

The belief that magical power existed in alloys and metals and that it could be manipulated, along with knowledge of the chemistry of the metals and their magical powers, was expressed by the name *Khemeia,* meaning "the preparation of the black ore (or powder)," which was regarded as the active principal in the transmutation of the metals.[11] To this, the Arabs affixed the prefix "al" producing the word *Al-Khemeia,* or alchemy, a linguistic coincidence that would perpetuate the reputation of Egyptians as successful students of both white magic and the black arts.[12]

Ethics of Magic

The magical arts of the Egyptians cannot be easily classified as white or black. Their magic consisted of two types: magical arts worked to benefit the living or the dead, and magic used with negative intent, such as throwing curses. The magician could heal the ailing or inflict ruin upon enemies. The balance of order and chaos could be tipped as willed. The justice or righteousness of these acts was determined by the individual. Egyptians used magic as deemed reasonable to protect and empower their livelihood.

As in every spiritual and magical system, the intent of the practitioner determines the magic worked, for good or evil. In situations that challenge our judgment, morals, and ethics, we attempt to act carefully. Our determination is solely our own, for no matter what course of action we take, there will always be individuals who agree or disagree with it. This is a basic tenet of Egyptian magic.

Action that is taken in response to life's trials and tribulations cannot always be analyzed and classified

---

[11] E. A. Wallis Budge, *Egyptian Magic,* p. 20.

[12] E. A. Wallis Budge, *Egyptian Magic,* p. 21.

as positive or negative, white or black. There is a gray realm that demands consideration for its potential consequences.

Like ancient magicians, you possess the ability to create or destroy. Acting responsibly, through faith and wisdom, you must contemplate the effects and consequences your magic will cause. This is the reason Egyptian magic is considered complex and potent, because it forces you to define yourself, discover mysteries within, and face the dark areas of your personality requiring transformation.

To work any form or system of magic is to open yourself to further lessons of a spiritual and Earthly nature. Aspiration to the magical arts is never to be taken lightly.

Sacred Mathematics

The origin of sacred geometry, mathematics, and astronomy may, in fact, have roots in Egypt. From an unknown source in the south, the Nile River coursed through Egypt. The Nile provided essential irrigation for agriculture. Every year it overflowed its banks and flooded the land, spreading beneficial fertile soil upon the land and irrigating crops. This annual flooding also caused crisis, however. The inundation helped to found the science of mathematics by creating a situation in which the land had to be resurveyed each time the waters receded; "geometry" literally means "land measurement."[13] It also led to the practical application of astronomy, since the annual inundation caused by tropical rainfall in the far south coincided with a particular configuration of stars in the sky.[14] The Egyptians called the star that forewarned of this phenomenon Sirius, the Dogstar. Sirius rose over the horizon in the northern sky, foretelling the upcoming flood.

---

[13] Gareth Knight, *Magic and the Western Mind* (St. Paul, MN: Llewellyn, 1991), p. 29.

[14] Gareth Knight, *Magic and the Western Mind,* p. 29.

Influence of Fate and Destiny

The Egyptians' magic was influenced by their beliefs concerning fate and destiny. A person's fate and destiny, they held, was decided before birth, and the individual had no power to change either. Sages could define what an individual's fate was, if told the date of the person's birth and the position of stars and planets at that time. In fact, we know that Egyptians practiced divination in many forms. (You will learn divination in chapter 5.) We also know that sages were considered powerful enough to work magic to change fate or destiny, whereas average Egyptians believed that they personally could not.

The goddess of fate or destiny was called "Shai." She is usually accompanied by a goddess "Renenet," who is commonly regarded as the lady of fortune. Together, these two goddesses appear in the famous Egyptian Judgment Scene, where they seem to watch the weighing of the heart on behalf of the deceased.[15] In chapter 5 you will explore working with these goddesses in your practice.

Ancient Egyptian religious and magical practices have influenced many philosophers, individuals, religions, and magical organizations in more recent times. The Hermetic tradition, the Rosicrucians, Freemasonry, witchcraft, and many other organized traditions have incorporated Egyptian symbols and ideas into their practice. No matter what religion or magical path you follow, you will discover Egyptian influence in some form.

Egyptian Temples

Learning the structure and operation of their ancient temples will help you understand how the Egyptians conducted both worship and magic. This will assist in

---

[15] E. A. Wallis Budge, *Egyptian Magic,* p. 222.

your preparation of sacred space for modern Egyptian magical practice. You will learn the traditions practiced in the ancient temples, and develop ideas of how your temple can be organized and decorated.

If you desire to form a modern-day Egyptian magical order, the following information can provide you with innovative ideas on how to structure the temple and form a hierarchy of priests and priestesses. Books listed in the bibliography can offer further details on the life and work of the ancient Egyptian priesthood.

Temple Structure

Egyptian temples symbolized the Earth. They were magnificent. The temples were sacred sites of both religious worship and awesome magic. The picture-writing that still remains on the ruins of their buildings once shone with vibrant hand-painted colors. Imagine walking into a shrine supported by great pillars with detailed lotus capitals and topped with rows of uraei (carved cobras).

Early Egyptian temples were made of mud and reeds. Later they were made of mud and brick, with windows and doorways made of stone. Ultimately, stone was used to construct the entire temple.

Unlike the Christian churches or Jewish synagogues we know of, Egyptian temples were important organizations in the community. The temple acted as a landlord and the average Egyptian rented land from it. They also served in much the same way as modern-day libraries and town halls, housing records of births, deaths, legal activities, and other documents. Business transactions were written up in the temple and both local and foreign trade was conducted there. Doctors, craftspeople, and scribes studied at temples. Some temples were used for funeral ceremonies for the dead, while others were dedicated to the worship of gods. Certain temples even housed the sick, since doctors were also priesthood members.

The temples were called the houses, or mansions, of whichever local or universal god or goddesses they served: for instance, the House of Heru. This naming convention reflects the Egyptians' domestic values. These houses contained rooms for eating and sleeping. The main sanctuary was considered the master bedroom for the god/goddess, and all other sanctuaries within were "guest rooms" for lesser deities. Each god lived in peace in his home, the temple, very often as part of a trinity of deities, a holy family consisting of father, mother, and child.[16]

Animals, birds, and reptiles were kept inside temples and revered as physical manifestations of the deities they represented. When these creatures died, each was mummified and buried in the same manner as royalty. Another important function of the temple was to protect and care for the gods so they could have maximum vitality for pursuing victory in the unseen, constant war between order and chaos.

Worship at the temples was more or less an exchange of favors between the Egyptian priest and the deity. For example, if the Pharaoh offered the god wine, the god in turn rewarded the Pharaoh with the gift of vineyards that produced the wine; if the royal offering were incense, the god promised the Pharaoh dominion over the land whence the incense came.[17] The Egyptians were spiritual people with high moral standards who revered their gods, but the worship between themselves and their deities was simple and direct. Only during special ceremonies were lengthy praises spoken. What we know as prayers were represented by the hieroglyphic wall carvings with which the Egyptians adorned their temples.

---

[16] Barbara Watterson, *Gods of Ancient Egypt*, p. 26.

[17] Barbara Watterson, *Gods of Ancient Egypt*, p. 40.

Making Your Own Temple

Egyptians practiced personal worship and had shrines in their homes. You can create a temple within your home or outside. In building a shrine or altar in your home or a sanctuary outdoors, include statues of the deities which intrigue you most. Decorate walls and furnishings with hieroglyphs. You can carve or paint hieroglyphs directly on these items, or draw them on papyrus and large stones to place in your temple. The possibilities for decoration and design of your personal sanctuary are limitless. There is no right or wrong design of a temple, sanctuary, or personal altar. Discover the symbols, images, objects, and figures that are a reflection of your own beliefs, or those that are magically appealing to you, and decorate as you desire.

It is important that your chosen incense, statuary, draperies, and altar produce a realm in which you are able to separate yourself from the material/mundane world. The images, symbols, and decorations of your temple area should serve as objects on which to focus your mind. They should help ensure that meditation, visualization, concentration, shape-shifting, and raising and directing energy are all done properly. You can best listen to, speak to, and interpret your unconscious mind through these factors. Your unconscious mind is opened to work magic through the language it understands best—images and symbols. In chapter 6 you will learn more about the importance of images and symbols in magic.

Temple Hierarchy

Egyptian temples were restricted to magicians and members of the priesthood. A priesthood's size depended upon the size of the town, and the importance of the temple or deity it served. The priests were divided into "gangs"; there were four gangs in each temple, each serving one lunar month in four during their years of service in the temple.[18] There were permanent and temporary members of the priesthood. One permanent member was the High Priest.

The Pharaoh and a hierarchy of priests used the temple to offer favors to the gods and receive favors in return. Since the Pharaoh was recognized as a god, he was also recognized as the chief priest of every temple. This meant he was the official who directed temple rituals and had entrance to the most holy spaces within. As he could not possibly be in every temple at once, there were chief priests to officiate in his absence.

The Pharaoh was recognized as the living connection between humankind and the gods. He had the extreme responsibility of making the world operate as needed; for causing the Nile to flood and recede, and agriculture to prosper. Yet, all of the Pharaoh's responsibilities were considered possible only if correct rituals were conducted within the temples.

The Temple and Citizenry

The average Egyptian was not permitted entrance inside a temple. Commoners recognized the local temple deities, mythology, functions, and the titles and duties of priesthood members. To them, priesthood members were community organizers, harmonizers, and neighbors. The relationship between the temple and community was similar to our relationship with the Pope. We know the title, duties, and some of the ritual tools of the Pope, but we are not permitted entrance to the Vatican or access to Vatican literature.

Egyptian citizens had religious shrines in their homes. They worshiped personal gods, which may or may not have been the same as their temple deities. Magic was also practiced by the average citizen.

---

18 Barbara Watterson, *Gods of Ancient Egypt*, p. 39.

It is thought that folk magic was practiced by them because the elaborate ceremonies of temples and magicians were unknown.

The community ceremonies, festivals, and pageants performed by the local priesthood had great meaning to citizens. Commoners were not merely bystanders at temple and priesthood public activities. Although they were not permitted to enter the temple, they called on temple officials as advisors, magicians, healers, state figures, and more.

Although the average Egyptian knew that elaborate funeral ceremonies were performed in the temple, as well as the process of mummification, the written magic recited at such ceremonies was kept from citizens. Temple training and ceremony was hidden from the public and holy books were kept secret in temple libraries.

Personal worship and magical practices were not spontaneous constructions. Common laborers built the obelisks, huge statues, temples, and sacred structures of Egypt. The craftsmen who painted and carved the picture-writing on the sacred architecture were citizens. To do so accurately, they had to be literate and understand what was written. Spells to ward off unworldly and worldly enemies, as well as other magical scripts written on buildings, were common knowledge to these craftsmen. This allowed citizens to participate to a certain extent in certain temple spells.

Likewise, merchants and farmers provided temples with supplies, and so learned what ritual items the priesthood used and why. How the ritual items were actually employed in those ceremonies were likely unknown, however.

Traditions were remembered and passed on by written and oral communication. They were woven into fables and historical accounts of the gods and humankind. Fables were told to children. Historical accounts reminded adults of the origin and legacy of Egyptian culture. Therefore, temple attendance was unnecessary. The average Egyptian had some knowledge of these traditions and exercised his freedom to worship and seek favor from preferred deities.

Ancient Initiates

It is vital that you become educated in the authentic role of an Egyptian priest or priestess. You need to know how priests and priestesses worked and what their responsibilities were. This will assist you in bringing new life to their ancient practices through your personal magical work.

If you plan to organize an authentic Egyptian magical order, you must be informed of the traditional priesthood operations. Some responsibilities discussed below, such as the leasing of land or the recording of a census, and some priesthood requirements, such as removal of all body hair for men, may not be practical for a modern order. Knowing these historical facts, however, will impress serious, prospective applicants seeking membership. The discipline, hierarchy, and provisions of the ancient Egyptian priesthoods provide building blocks to create a practicing Egyptian organization today.

The Pharaoh, as god manifest on Earth, appointed the priests and priestesses of a temple. There were politics in the priesthood. The Pharaoh was able to appoint whomever he chose. If the man or woman could live with whatever prohibitions existed, they accepted. Two requirements for the priesthood were to be in good standing with the Pharaoh (or an official) and to be pure.

For a man or a woman to become a member of the priesthood, purification was mandatory. Initiates had to smudge and breathe in incense and chew natron. On the day of entry, they had to bathe, cut their finger- and toe-nails, and, in the case of a priest, be circumcised, shaved, and depilated of all body hair.[19] Priesthood members were faced with restrictions in their daily living, such as not eating fish. Each temple had its own prohibitions.

In return, priesthood members were granted many benefits. They were exempt from some taxes, did not have to serve as laborers, had a share from temple income, and their immediate relatives could have a specified share of the temple revenues.

Rarely are priestesses mentioned in papyri, or in any books written by Egyptologists, but they did exist. Women were regular members of priesthoods. The lady Thuthu, wife of the royal scribe Ani, who wrote the *Papyrus of Ani*, belonged to the number of priestesses of the god Amen-Ra at Thebes. She carried in her hands the sistrum and the instrument menat, the emblems of her office.[20]

Members of the priesthood served a specific time in the temple and then were free to go home and lead their usual lives. There were scribes who were priests, and priests who practiced magic. Magicians did not exist as a separate sect.

Priesthood Titles

Not all the titles and positions assigned to priesthood members are known. The following ten examples demonstrate an ancient Egyptian priesthood that is known to have performed funeral ceremonies:[21]

1. The *Kher-heb*, or chief officiating priest, who held a roll of papyrus in his hand.
2. The *Sem* priest, whose function is not entirely known.
3. The *Smer*, who was, perhaps, an intimate friend of the deceased.

---

19 Barbara Watterson, *Gods of Ancient Egypt*, p. 38.

20 E. A. Wallis Budge, *Egyptian Book of the Dead*, p. cxlv.

21 E. A. Wallis Budge, *Egyptian Magic*, pp. 192–193.

4. The *Sa-mer-ef* (meaning "the son who loveth him"), a man who was the son of the deceased, or his representative.
5. The *Tcherau-ur,* a woman or priestess who represented Auset.
6. The *Tcherau-sheraut,* a woman or priestess who represented Nebt-het.
7. The *Menhu,* or slaughter. It is thought the Menhu acted as a butcher preparing food as an offering.
8. The *Am-asi* priest, who assisted the Sem priest.
9. The *Am-khent* priest. Duty unknown.
10. A number of people who represented the armed guard Heru.

The priesthood members above conducted funerary ceremonies. They enacted the "awakening" of the deceased's many bodies. It is believed they were regular priesthood members who performed other religious and magical ceremonies as well. It is unknown if their titles changed for other temple work.

Priestesses, bore the Egyptian title *qematet,* represented by this hieroglyph . They were considered part of the elite, members of the upper class of Egyptian society. The word *rekhet* has been found in a few personal letters of the second millennium B.C. It refers to a woman as a "knowing one."[22] Such women were employed to contact the dead, diagnose sick children, and possibly to work as seers.

The word *Sau* is a form of the Egyptian verb *sa,* "to protect." It defines both wise men and women who practiced medicine and magic. This word is among the many titles that such men and women held. Other titles include priest, amulet man, magician, and scorpion charmer.

---

22 Geraldine Pinch, *Magic in Ancient Egypt* (Austin, TX: University of Texas Press, 1995), p. 56.

Priesthood Duties

Priests/priestesses were not trained in religious law, or as spiritual providers to the people. There was no congregation to lead. The men or women appointed as members were chosen because of their ability to oversee temple property and transactions. Priests and priestesses became servants to the god(s) of the temple, which meant caring for the living creature residing in the temple as the deity manifested upon the Earth. Duties were likely assigned by the Chief Priest. Individual responsibilities were probably determined by personal talents, abilities, and education.

Priests and priestesses represented specific deities in the temple. Individual duties in ceremonies likely depended on the characteristics of the deity represented. A priestess of Sekhmet probably performed defensive magic against enemies threatening war, while priests of Tehuti perhaps served as scribes of magical scripts.

The priesthood assisted the local community. They healed the ailing with medicine and magic, removed evil magic and spirits from those in need, scryed to obtain unknown answers for seekers, and performed other magical tasks. It is not known if fees were charged for such services.

Priesthood Dress

Practicing Egyptian magic cannot be complete without learning of the proper ritual attire to be worn. The descriptions below include simple instructions for making the clothing, following designs researched by scholars, anthropologists, and curators of Egyptian antiquities. You can make your own Egyptian priest or priestess attire easily, with little effort or expense.

For the most part, Egyptian royalty dressed conservatively. White and off-white linen, the very finest called *byssos,* was used for royal and priestly robes, drapes for shrines, and statues of gods. Through trading, they acquired wool and leather. In Roman times, they had access to Chinese silk. In the Coptic period, cotton and mohair came into their possession.

White and off-white linen was the preferred choice for clothing. The Egyptians dyed fabric by using traditional plant dyes, for instance, safflower for the colors yellow and red. Loops and details composed of thread, much like embroidery, were used to create patterns in the fabric. Colored and detailed fabrics were for royalty and the priesthood.

Clothing of Male Royalty and Priests: Egyptian men wore kilts. Made from a rectangular length of linen folded around the body and tied at the waist, or else fastened with a sort of buckle, the kilt reached to the knee and was worn universally without regard to status or class.[23] (See figure 1, page 26.) For undergarments, both men and women wore triangular loincloth underwear.

The kilt was sometimes enhanced by pleating. Its ends could be rounded or squared. High officials, including priests, wore long kilts that extended from their underarm/chest to their calf, or even to their ankles.

On the *Narmer Palette* and other royal documents of the archaic period, Pharaohs are depicted wearing a form of the kilt made of a rectangle of cloth longer than was usual later, long enough that the ends could be pulled diagonally across the torso and knotted on one shoulder. This early item of clothing is shown in later carvings and art being worn by the male gods. Later, the "bag tunic" was introduced. It consisted of a rectangle of cloth folded and sewn up the sides to form a sleeveless garment that was worn tied with a sash.[24]

---

[23] L. Green, "Seeing Through Ancient Egyptian Clothes," *K*M*T* Magazine: A Modern Journal of Ancient Egypt*, vol. 6. No. 4, Winter 1995–1996, p. 36.

[24] L. Green, "Seeing Through Ancient Egyptian Clothes," pp. 36 and 37.

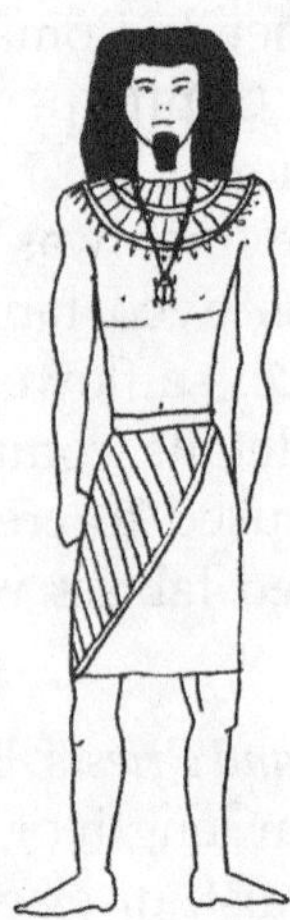

Figure l. Kilt with broad collar, wig, and amulet pendant.

At times, in the Middle Kingdom, a cloak, fringed or unfringed, pleated or unpleated, was worn with the kilt. During festivals or on other important occasions, pleated cloaks and semi-transparent, finely woven linen tunics and wrappings were worn. The wrappings were nothing more than large fabric pieces that draped the body. Royalty and the more notable priests wore what was called a sed-festival cloak and shendyt-kilt.

Sem-priests were known to wear an entire leopard pelt over one shoulder as part of their sacerdotal attire.[25] Furs and whole animal skins were common accessories to priestly garments (see figure 2, page 27).

Because the Pharaoh had many priestly roles, his wardrobe also contained a number of abstruse items: kilts, cloaks, transparent shawls, colorful gloves, beaded and tapestry-woven tunics, socks with a single toe (like Japanese *tabi*), and sleeves with "wings," not

---

[25] L. Green, "Seeing Through Ancient Egyptian Clothes," p. 28.

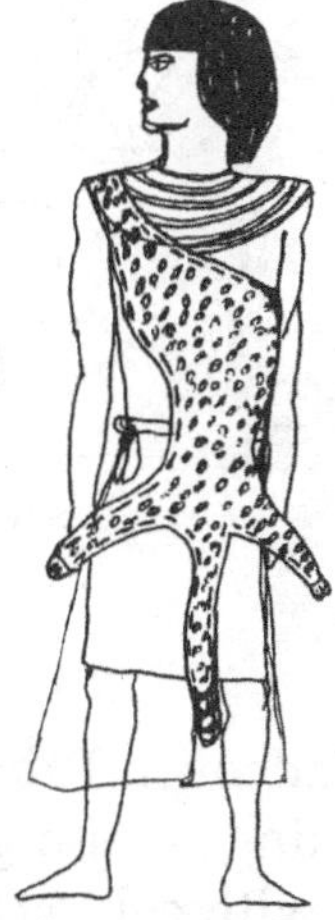

Figure 2. Sem priest wearing leopard pelt, priest wig, collar, kilt, and sheer kilt.

to mention faux-leopard skins, aprons, belts and "tails" of beadwork and gold.[26] We can assume that other members of the priesthood wore similar items, as the Pharaoh could not be present as the chief priest in every temple.

Like Egyptian women, most men and officials wore beaded collars and many times, necklaces with a single handmade amulet pendant, as well as armbands that were engraved with protective spells, words to bring good fortune, and deities. Intricate snake armbands, made of bronze and other metals, were worn on the upper arm and looped around the arm two or three times. Wide bracelets were worn by both sexes as well, and royalty often had their cartouches engraved on them.

Men wore black wigs that revealed their ears. These were first made of animal hair and later of human hair. The Pharaoh wore a *nemes,* which was a headcover,

[26] L. Green, "Seeing Through Ancient Egyptian Clothes," p. 39.

Figure 3. Nemes headcover. Fabric, pleated, white or off-white, worn by kings and high officials or priests. Often adorned with cobra ornament on top.

probably made of white or off-white pleated linen. (See figure 3.)

How to Make a Nemes: You will need 1 yard of ivory linen or white/ivory cotton fabric, measuring tape, scissors, a sewing needle and thread or a sewing machine, 1 wide ribbon of any color or two matching fabric thongs.

1. Measure your forehead across, and partially down to the nape of your neck. Cut the material in a truncated pyramid shape, so that the top is two inches larger than your head measurement and has a narrow edge, and the bottom has a wide edge.
2. Cut about a 45-degree angle from each end of the top to the bottom edge (see figure 4, page 29). The distance from the top of the nemes to the bottom should be about fifteen inches.
3. Make approximately a 3/4-inch hem all around the nemes.

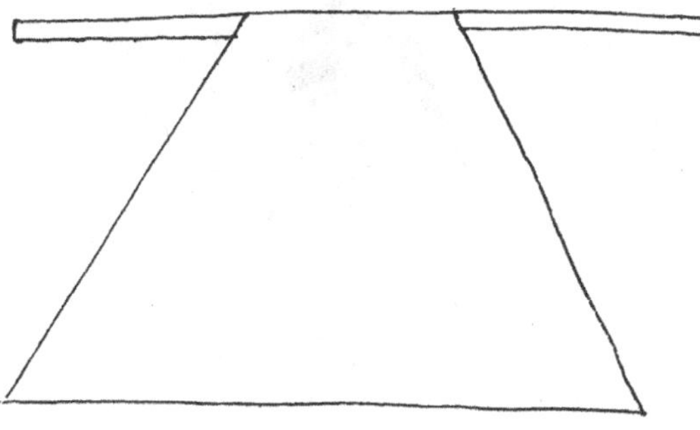

Figure 4. Nemes pattern.

4. Sew a wide ribbon or a matching fabric thong to each side of the top of the nemes.
5. The nemes is worn by placing its top edge against your forehead and securing the ties around to the back of your head, at the nape of your neck beneath the nemes.

Clothing of Female Royalty and Priestesses: Elite women and priestesses wore an unpleated inner robe and sheer fabric beneath an outer, draped robe made of the finest byssos. Due to the Egyptian acceptance of the human body in its natural form, it appears that women's breasts were rarely covered by clothing.

Common and upper-class women, priestesses, and queens also wore the loose-fitting, long, linen "sheath dress" from the time of the Old Kingdom to the New Kingdom. This dress was held up by thin straps that passed bet ween the breasts. Upper-class women sometimes wore broader straps that covered the breasts. There were two other versions of this garment; one sleeveless with two straps over each shoulder, and one long-sleeved, which appears to fit much like a long-sleeved, simple dress of today. The sheath dresses were probably formed from a rectangle of linen material folded lengthwise and sewn down one side, then

Figure 5. Priestess/royalty wrapped gown.

hemmed, with a pair of broad straps added to go over the shoulders of the wearer.[27]

Priestesses' clothing reflected what royal ladies wore. While some articles of clothing were common to all classes of people, there were garments that only royalty could afford to enjoy. Priestesses and affluent ladies of about 1350 B.C., attending festivals or important gatherings wore sleeveless wrapped gowns, that were likely not sewn, but consisted rather of long, rectangular pieces of white linen wrapped loosely around the body twice, then tied in the front and over one shoulder, leaving the other shoulder bare. Fringe was sometimes added to one short side. A long shawl or draped cloak might have been added to the outfit (see figure 5).

Extraordinary bead-net dresses appear in the 12th Dynasty that were made of mitra shells and other colorful

---

[27] Rita E. Freed, *Egypt's Golden Age* (Boston: Museum of Fine Arts, 1982) see "costume."

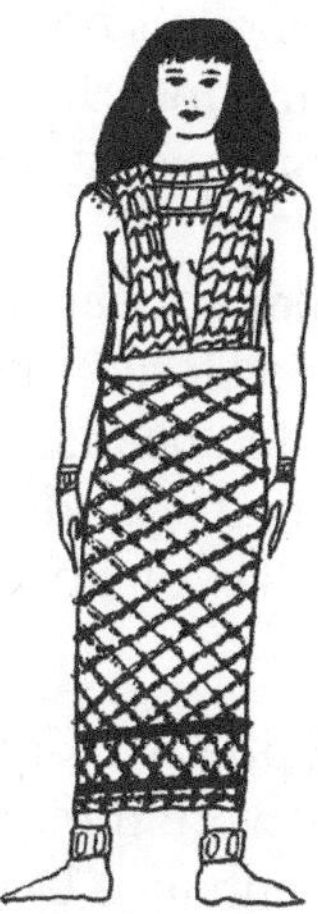

Figure 6. Bead-net dress over sheath dress.

bead-like materials. These were worn either over a sleeveless linen sheath dress or alone, with nipple cups sewn into the garment. Figure 6 shows a bead-net dress worn over a sheath dress.

Priestesses and other women wore beaded headbands, beaded collars, large gold earrings, and wigs. It is not known if priestesses wore elaborate headpieces during ceremonies. If they did, these may have been beaded headbands with a golden serpent or other ornament depicting the goddess represented.

Making Beaded Collars and Headbands: Although beaded collars and decorated headbands require some preparation, patience, and effort, you can purchase beads and supplies from a craft shop to make your own. Cylinder and disk faience beads, mitra shells, lapis lazuli, turquoise, carnelian, and various other colored stones can be used effectively to create an Egyptian collar or headband. Any wire or thread can be used to secure the beads and ornaments. In Egypt, gold wire was used to make delicate circlets and crowns. Copper wire can be used today. As we are uncertain of the correct method for making these pieces of jewelry, you will need to use your own creativity.

The traditional collar appears to have consisted of multiple strands of beads and stones made to form a broad collar. Single strings of threaded beads and stones were connected together by short, knotted strands of thread. Use your imagination to design a collar or headband that is unique and personally yours.

Wigs: The ancient Egyptians wore wigs daily as well as for ceremonies. The wigs were thought to be both fashionable and practical, and to enhance beauty. Different wigs were worn for special occasions.

Exactly why Egyptians chose to wear wigs is unknown. There are two theories. One suggests that the hot climate made it more comfortable for them to shave their natural hair and wear wigs instead. The other is that the Egyptians were very vain and desired to conceal all signs of aging. Of course, styled wigs would hide gray hair.

Egyptian wigs were handmade, but the process by which they were made is not known. The first wigs were made out of animal hair; later, human hair was used. In the Old Kingdom, the animal-hair wigs were thick, straight, shoulder length, and worn low on the brow. Short wigs did exist, but were not the popular choice.

In the New Kingdom, women wore human-hair wigs that were made lavishly full, and were braided, curled, or frizzed. Men chose to wear heavy, shoulder-length wigs that were styled in two layers. At the bottom of the men's wig was a row of ringlets. Men wore wigs that showed their ears; women wore wigs that covered their ears. Priests did not wear wigs, as one of their prohibitions was against body hair. The priests had shaven heads. It is not clear whether priestesses wore their heads shaved or not.

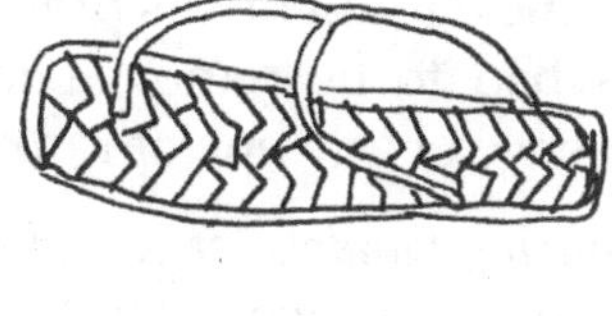

Figure 7. Rush-work sandals.

Purchasing a Costume Wig: Wigs are readily available today. You can purchase a black wig similar to an Egyptian wig. An African-American heavily braided wig is ideal. Any mail-order wig catalog, and most beauty supply shops, have several wig styles from which to choose. Wigs are a fun, authentic addition to your Egyptian attire. As it is not known how Egyptian wigs were made and the materials needed in wig manufacture are not readily available, it may be best for you to purchase a wig.

Egyptian Footwear: Sandals were popular footwear in ancient Egypt and are thought to have been available to all social classes. The less expensive sandals were made of grass and reed. The more expensive sandals were made of leather and rawhide. In later times, sandals were even gilded, beaded, and painted. The soles of a pair of rawhide sandals in the Metropolitan Museum of Art are formed from thick rawhide cut to the approximate size and shape of each foot, with a loop of rawhide projecting upward on either side of the ankle and a third rawhide loop extending upward between the first and second toes. Through these loops runs a leather strap that passes behind the heel and over the instep.[28] (See figure 7.)

---

[28] L. Green, "Seeing Through Ancient Egyptian Clothes," p. 32.

Ancient Egyptians preferred to be barefoot. In fact, sandals had to be removed immediately when entering the presence of any one of rank.

Acquiring Sandals for Ritual Use: You can decide either to go barefoot or to wear sandals in your sacred space. Sandals are important to protect your feet if you practice your magic outdoors, but otherwise they are optional.

Although the construction and design of Egyptian sandals are described above, the raw materials to make them are not readily available. Making the sandals is very difficult. There are Egyptian supply catalogs listed in the Egyptian Resources section, some of which may sell reproductions of the sandals. You can always purchase a pair at any shoe store that will work just as well.

You are now able to visualize what an Egyptian priest and priestess wore during their services. In portraying the ancient priesthoods, you can recreate the splendid ceremony and mysticism of ancient Egyptian practices. With an understanding of Egyptian religious and magical philosophy, the functions of the temple, the hierarchy of the priesthood, and the ritual clothing, you have the basics needed to begin the exciting journey into Egyptian magic.

Chapter Two

Ritual Tools

un-sen uat enen pert em re-k
They open the ways [for] that
which cometh forth from thy mouth.

Artifacts found and identified in tombs have offered us knowledge of many of the magical items used by royalty and priesthoods. The work of archaeologists and Egyptologists allows us to recreate of the magical tools that flourished in ancient Egypt. The treasures found in tombs had spiritual and magical purpose. Many were used by both the living and the dead.

In this chapter you will learn of many ritual tools—divination and magical tools such as magical figures, pictures, oils, and statues. You can make them for your personal use. Illustrations and instructions will help you to make them correctly. This chapter also defines magical implements, which you have the freedom of using as desired. You will learn their Egyptian use in the divination and magical formulas of chapter 5 and chapter 6. There was no manual of strict use for any particular ritual tool in Egypt.

The best-known ritual tools are associated with funeral ceremonies, as described in *The Egyptian Book of the Dead.*

The tools described below were used by the living, as described in ancient magical papyri. Egyptologists and researchers learned from papyri that many implements were used in religious and magical ceremonies. We do not know, however, precisely how each was used. As there is no way to be certain of traditional use, you must use your own intuition and creativity.

Divination Tools

Egyptians scryed primarily by fire, oil, and/or water. Additional items that had symbolic value to the magician were incorporated into the rituals. Some tools have no known definition or understood purpose, however. Below, a definition and purpose of each tool is provided, followed by instructions for making or obtaining the tool.

Oil Lamp

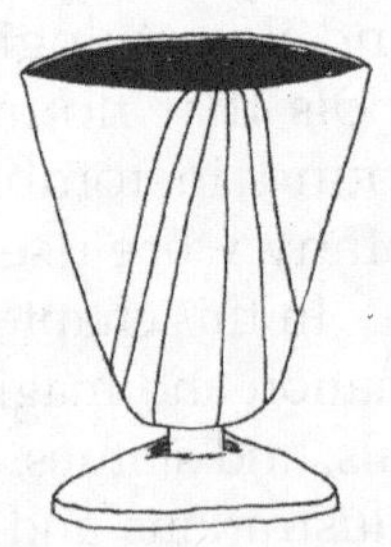

The Egyptian magician favored divination by lamp. Divination lamps were required to be white and free from any red color,[1] although earthenware and terra cotta lamps of red color were used to make offerings and served other purposes in magic. The white divination lamps were made of various substances. Alabaster, finished to a beautiful, smooth white surface, was a popular substance. In certain divination formulas, bronze lamps were indicated.

Lamps were always used in dark, secret places. Only clean wicks were used, and real oil was placed inside the lamp. By Egyptian rule, the lamps were forbidden to touch the ground, so they were often set upon crude

[1] F. L. Griffith and Herbert Thompson, eds., *The Leyden Papyrus: An Egyptian Magical Book* (New York: Dover, 1974), p. 44.

bricks on the ground. Magicians sat before the lamp or bent over it to fire scry. Scribes often gave helpful hints in their formulas: one such hint was for the magician to lie down on a reed mat before the lamp, with his head to the south and his face turned to the north, along with the lamp.

Another option was to fill the lamp with oil, tie it with four threads of linen, and hang it on a peg of bay wood on an eastern wall in the room in which magic would be worked.[2] The magician would then insert a clean wick, light it, and stand before the lamp for divination.

A lamp of this type would be difficult for you to make or obtain. You can purchase a simple oil lamp, however, that has a round vessel to hold the oil and apparatus at its mouth to insert a linen wick. Linen for wicks is available at many fabric stores. A more modern oil lamp—with a hurricane chimney—would also work very well.

Vessel

A clean bronze cup or a new vessel of pottery was traditionally used. This was filled with water and, once the water settled, Oasis or vegetable oil was poured on top of the water. Oil was also used alone. The vessel was often used in conjunction with the lamp. The lamp shed light upon the oil when divination was conducted in a private, dark place.

Vessels of bronze are not common today, but they can be purchased at stores carrying fine china dishes and other household accessories. Pottery vessels are easier to acquire. To make your own, you can visit any craft shop for a pottery kit. There are clay and earthenware kits available, and some can be baked in your home oven.

---

2 F. L. Griffith and Herbert Thompson, eds., *The Leyden Papyrus,* Col. XXVII, p. 159.

Bowl

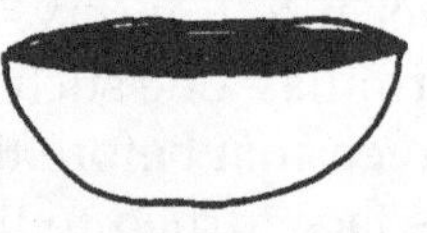

The bowl was used the same way as the vessel. Most were made of bronze and were frequently used with water for scrying. A figure of the god or goddess invoked in divination was often engraved inside the bronze bowl. Typically, this was the god Anpu. Words of power and magical names were often engraved on the outside of bowls. To use a bowl in divination, you need to understand a piece of Egyptian history regarding its use: Of all the Egyptians skilled in working magic, Nectanebus, the last native king of Egypt (c. B.C. 358), was the best known—at least, if we may believe Greek tradition.[3] His works were translated into Arabic, Syriac, Pehlevi, and many other languages and dialects. Famous as a magician and a sage, Nectanebus was deeply versed in Egyptian lore. He was adept at interpreting omens, sending created dreams to other individuals, procuring dreams, casting nativities, predicting the future of an unborn child, and in all magic. Indeed, he was considered a lord of the Earth, able to rule all kings by his magical powers. He created divination and magical script using a bowl of water. Unfortunately, no texts survive to state the material of which the bowl was made.

Nectanebus used the bowl of water in magic to defeat enemies, arriving by ship. He made wax figures of both enemy ships and men, and his own, then uttered invocations of the gods, winds, and subterranean demons. His wax figures came to life and battled. As enemy figures sank to the bottom of the bowl, Nectanebus thought his enemies would descend to the bottom of the sea. And in fact, he was successful in defeating many enemies and reigning for a considerable period of time.

---

3 E. A. Wallis Budge, *Egyptian Magic* (New York: Dover, 1971), p. 91.

From descriptions in E. A. Wallis Budge's *Egyptian Magic*, we learn how Nectanebus prepared for his magical work. He retired to a private chamber and retrieved the bowl, which he kept especially for such purpose. He filled the bowl with water, put on the cloak of an Egyptian prophet, and held an ebony rod in his hand. Thereafter, the script was recited and the magic work done.

Bricks

Egyptian bricks were crude and were used as the principal building material, as well as in divination. The bricks were set upon the ground and were used as a base for the lamp, vessel, or bowl. Sand was sprinkled under the bricks for purification and to add magical influence. The magician often sat on a brick while scrying. When another person, a medium, was used as the seer during divination, the medium would sit on bricks and the magician would recite the formula over his or her head.

Researchers are uncertain why the Egyptians felt it necessary to have both the scrying tool and the seer positioned off the ground. It is known that the priesthoods and magicians were extremely disciplined concerning purity in all magical work. That alone may be the reason. Later, burned bricks, introduced by the Romans in Byzantine times, were used for the same purpose.

You can easily purchase a couple of new bricks rather than attempting to make them. Home and building centers carry a variety of bricks. Sand, gravel, and stone dealers can be found in your telephone book yellow pages and may offer a selection, usually at better prices.

Censer

Censers were often used in worship, divination, and magic in Egypt. Clay, earthenware, or bronze censers (or braziers) held burning incense. Olive-wood charcoal was used to burn the incense.

Today, you can purchase a censer made of these materials, or you can handcraft your own clay censer by purchasing a kit sold in craft stores. Olive wood is difficult to obtain, but may be found through herb farms or herb mail-order companies. The charcoal tablets commonly sold in New Age shops will work as a substitute.

Incense

Egyptians traded for and purchased their incense from a town called Punt, near Somalia. Egyptian priests and magicians used different types of incense, but frankincense and myrrh were preferred. Ancient incense was used in resin form only. Incense sticks and cones were not used. You can buy resin incense today from New Age shops and mail-order companies. (See Egyptian Resources, page 217.)

Oil

Egyptians found that oil was better for scrying than water alone because its surface did not distort easily and disrupt the magician's concentration. Cedar, Oasis, and vegetable oils were used for divination. Scribes suggested that the oil was added to the dish gradually to avoid it becoming cloudy. The oil had to be as clear and free of debris as possible.

Cedar oil is made from the dried wood. Today, the Atlas cedar and red cedar are used to make essential oil. The oil can be found at any shop selling essential oils or herbs. You need a lot of it for scrying, so it may be costly. (NOTE: Pregnant women should not use cedar oil). Vegetable oil is readily available to you and can be found in your local grocery store.

Oasis is described in papyri as "real oil," however, no other definition is given. The word *oasis* describes a place in the desert that is fertile due to the presence of water. It may be that standing water that had absorbed minerals and plant debris over time was taken from such places in Egypt. The debris would have given the water an oily texture.

Eye-Paint

This liquid was handmade and placed into the eyes in order to see the gods during divination. The Egyptians used several recipes—some including the blood or gall of particular animals, herbs, and plants. It is not known exactly how the eye-paint worked. It may have caused distorted vision, allowing the magician to see deities, beings, or creatures conjured in divination and magic. There may also have been a drug effect in certain recipes.

How to Make Greek Bean Eye-Paint: In magical papyri, there are several recipes for making eye-paint. Most recipes are not practical or considered safe for our use today. One such recipe involves pounding a hawk's egg with natural myrrh (not incense). Obviously, both ingredients are not easily obtained today and knowledge of how to properly make or store such a potion is unknown.

The recipe below is found in *The Leyden Papyrus*. The scribe who recorded the recipe wrote that it had been "tested" and was "excellent." You will need a supply of Greek bean plant, also known as "raven's eye." This can be found where lupine, a plant of the pea family, is sold. Usually, it can be purchased at herb farms, through herb retailers, and at some garden centers that sell vegetable seeds or plants.

1. Take the fresh flowers of the Greek bean plant and put them in a clean glass bottle. Stop the mouth of the bottle tightly and leave it in a secret dark place for twenty days.

2. After twenty days, remove the bottle and open it. You will find that the flowers resemble testicles with a phallus. Close the bottle tightly and leave it in the dark place for forty days.
3. When you open the bottle after forty days and look inside, you will find that the contents have become blood-colored. Your eye-paint is ready to use. You can leave the bloodlike liquid in this glass bottle, but it must be stored in a hidden place at all times.

Eye-paint is not necessary and was not always employed in divination. Before using this eye-paint, you should determine that you are not allergic to the plant.

Knots

Knot or cord magic, used in folk magic or early witchcraft, originated in Egypt. Instructions for these techniques are detailed in various magical papyrus.

How to Use Knots in Divination: In *The Leyden Papyrus*, Col. III, page 39, there are instructions for making an amulet of knots for the purpose of working divination and magic quickly. Because a live scarab is not easily obtained in our Western world, I have omitted its use in the instructions below. You will need 16 individual linen threads, each approximately a foot long (4 white, 4 green, 4 blue, and 4 red), and a drop of personal blood.

1. Take the 16 individual threads of linen and make them into one band.
2. Stain the band with a drop of your blood. Women can use menstrual blood. Be careful to use a sterilized pin or other instrument for drawing your blood.
3. Bind the band to some part of your body, such as your arm, before divination or magic. This amulet is to be bound to whomever has the vessel and wants it to work magic quickly.

Writing Ink

Many plant dyes and natural dyes were used as ink for writing on papyrus. A popular choice was the juniper plant, whose juice was a favorite of the Egyptians and the Greeks. A reed pen, made from the plant's shoots, was used to apply the writing inks. Reed pens are not practical today, although some companies in the appendix may supply them. Quill pens and sable paintbrushes are natural writing utensils that can be substituted. In chapter 3 you will learn how to make and use the tools of ancient scribes, including further information about writing ink.

Reed Mat

Reed mats were used primarily during worship for the priest or priestess to kneel upon, and during divination for the magician to sit or lie upon while communing with the gods or other invoked beings. After reciting the divination formula—through which a shift of consciousness occurred—in some instances, the magician would lie down on a reed mat in a trance state or fall asleep to receive answers to his or her inquiries.

Reed is actually a general term used to describe various types of grasses with jointed, hollow stems. Rustic musical pipes were made from the reed stem, and long strips of reed were woven together to make the ancient mats.

Making a reed mat takes great skill. Finding such a mat is very difficult. You may contact sources of Egyptian wares listed in the Egyptian Resources section of this book to find out if they can recommend a source for these mats today, or you can use a woven mat available commercially.

Kohl-Stick

Unfortunately, not much is known about this wooden ritual staff. In *The Leyden Papyrus* it is described as "the stick of satisfaction," which indicates its use in acquiring satisfying results in divination and magic. Col. XXIX, 1.27 of this same papyrus describes preparation instructions for a magician in which a kohl-pot and kohl-stick are used to pound together the ingredients of an herbal and organic potion. It is possible that the kohl-stick served as a pestle. In Col. X, there are instructions for the magician to bind the kohl-stick to his waist, and then to travel to an elevated place outdoors, in daylight, opposite the Sun, for Sun divination.

To make a kohl-stick, obtain a fallen tree branch to serve as a ritual staff. Strip the bark from it, and decorate it as desired.

Constellations

Astrology was practiced in Egypt as a practical and magical art. Egyptians observed that certain constellations were visible on the horizon at night, allowing them to tell time by the position of a particular constellation in the sky at a given hour. Scribes drew up tables that recorded the readings for the purpose of telling time and working magic.

The Shoulder constellation, also called "The Great Bear" in Egypt and known to the English-speaking world as Ursa Major, consists of seven stars. Since seven is a sacred Egyptian number, it is no wonder that this constellation was used in magic. From *The Leyden Papyrus*, we learn that, for best success, a divination formula was recited seven times, at night, opposite the Shoulder constellation, on the third day of the month.

The same papyrus instructs magicians to set up their divination materials in a dark recess, then venture outdoors into the night to stamp the ground with their foot seven times, and then recite the opening charms of any divination script to the Foreleg/Great Bear constellation. Then the magician must turn to the north seven times and retreat to the dark recess to begin the actual divination inquiry.

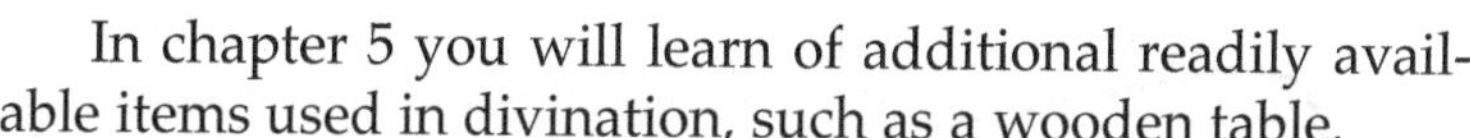

In chapter 5 you will learn of additional readily available items used in divination, such as a wooden table.

Tools for Magic

Tools used in divination were also used for magical work. Remember, the Egyptians considered divination to be magic, not a separate subject, as tends to be the case in contemporary practice. Ritual staffs, the sistrum, the menat, gold rings, water, figures, pictures, statues, minerals, wreaths, earthenware dishes, lamps, oils, and even constellations are used in both divination and magic. Some items, such as the menat, had symbolic uses and were meant to be held or carried by a priest, priestess, god, or king.

Ritual Staffs

In Egypt, there were not many trees, or many different types of trees, so wood was very valuable to them and highly regarded. Although there was an abundance of stone, wood was scarce. It was used to make magical rods and as the core of many statues. Egyptians traded with foreigners for exotic wood, which is probably why they delighted in making and using countless wooden ritual staffs.

Many sizes, shapes, and types of carvings were used in the manufacture. It is impossible to know the precise use for each staff or rod, but Egyptologists have gained ideas through deciphering hieroglyphs. One type, the Was-Scepter or Uas Staff, was traditionally made of heti wood. This staff was forked at the bottom and carved at the top to resemble the head of an animal. The top is often called a "canid," and resembles the god Anpu, with long carved ears.

There are pictorials of gods holding this staff. Ausar, as the night Sun, was always represented as a mummy

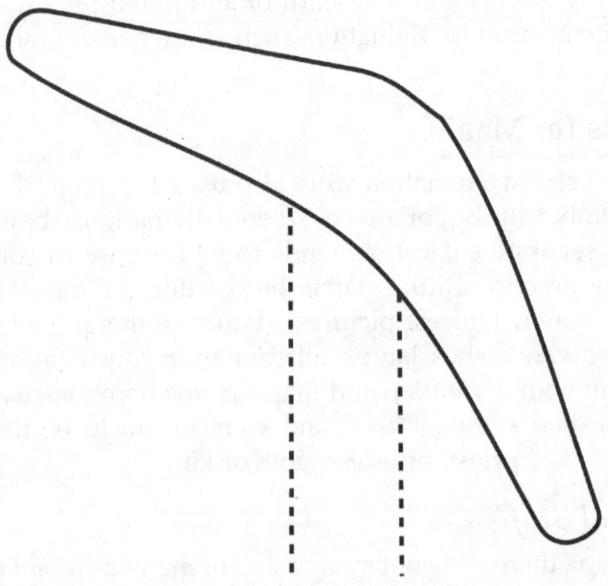

Figure 8. Animal head-shaped top of Uas staff.

holding the scepter, crook, and flail. The Uas staff is a staff of divinity and royalty. There are instances in which a priest is shown holding this staff, suggesting it was used in religious and magical ceremonies. It was not common for priestesses to carry this staff. Priestesses carried the sistrum and menat, which you will learn more about later in this section.

How to Make a Uas Staff: The Uas staff is not difficult to make. You will need a fresh tree branch (not rotted), approximately five feet long, with a forked bottom. It should be at least an inch and a half to two inches in diameter to allow you to carve the angle that supports the animal head at the top. In addition, you will need a rectangular piece of wood approximately six inches long and four inches wide, a pencil, a chisel, a hammer, a C-clamp or vise, a worktable, a hand saw (keyhole or coping), and wood glue.

1. Strip the bark from the tree branch and check it for rotted areas.
2. Secure the branch to a worktable using a C-clamp or a vise.
3. Use your chisel and hammer to chip wood at a 90-degree angle from one side of the staff top. This creates the angle upon which the animal head will be affixed. There is no right or wrong length for the angled surface. When finished, remove your staff from the worktable.
4. Take the smaller piece of wood and with the pencil, draw a narrow and simple animal head that consists of a long snout and two flattened ears. (See figure 8, page 46.)
5. Secure the wood with drawing to the worktable. Following your pattern, use a coping or keyhole saw to trim away the extra wood to form the animal head.
6. If desired, carve out a prominent groove between the two flattened ears using the chisel and hammer.
7. Remove the animal head from the worktable and secure your staff there. Affix the animal head to the staff's angled top with generously applied wood glue. Clamp the head into position and allow the glue to dry overnight.

Woodworking requires caution, time, and patience. Perfection is not necessary, so do not become frustrated.

When you have carved the design of the head, you have achieved the traditional appearance. You can use a small pocketknife to whittle finer details into the wood if desired.

Crook

This short wooden staff was held by gods, pharaohs, and certain priests, symbolizing sovereignty and dominion. Priests and priestesses both carried the crook during worship rituals, magical ceremonies, festivals, and other rites.

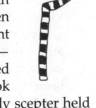

It was traditional for the crook to be held in the right hand of both royal and priestly men and women. Men held the crook in their right hand, usually holding the flail in their left—often in the Ausar position, with arms crossed over the chest. Priestesses held the crook casually at their right side and carried the lily scepter held against their chest with their left hand.[4]

Magician's Rod

This is a general term given to numerous short wooden staffs that were held in the left hand by magicians and priests when performing magical rites. The typical magician's rod was made of bronze, with one end finished in the fans and head of a cobra. The entire staff length depicts a cobra, representing the god of magic, Heka, or his female equivalent, the goddess Weret Hekau, who was usually shown in cobra form.[5] The god Heka is pictured in funerary papyri as a human man holding two of these snake-shaped rods crisscrossed over his chest, suggesting that the Egyptians thought highly of the rod's practical use.

Exactly how this rod was used in magical rites is unknown. We do know that these rods were used as emblems of the magician's control over the gods, creatures, and beings he invoked, or evoked, during magical work. Often consisting of glazed steatite, these rods were hollow and made in sections that were ingeniously fit together. The sides of the rod were decorated with lamps,

---

4 Lionel Casson, *The Pharaohs*, in *Treasures of the World Series* (Chicago: Stonehenge, 1981), p. 142.

5 Geraldine Pinch, *Magic in Ancient Egypt* (Austin, TX: University of Texas Press, 1995), p. 11.

baboons, crocodiles, lions, the Eye of Heru, and other protective symbols. The figure of a turtle, thought to be unclean but useful to protect against harmful forces, was likely attached to the top end of the rod. Presumably, the magician held control of the protective and aggressive power of the creatures decorating the rod to use as he desired.

In another example of the numerous magical rods employed by magicians, the last native-born ruler of Egypt, Nectanebo, waved an ebony rod to invoke gods and devils to defeat animated wax models of his enemies and their ships.

Lily Scepter

It is uncertain if this scepter, carried by ladies of royalty and priestesses, was an actual lily stem with flower, or made of wood. Certain pictorials of priestesses carrying the scepter suggest it was made of wood, while others show a leaning, flexible material that indicates the use of a real lily.

The lily scepter was held in the left hand of the priestess, and the crook was held in her right. She hugged the scepter to her chest as she walked through the temple and carried out her various duties and magic.

The process by which to make this scepter is unknown. You may choose to use a real lily in your magic. Lily bulbs are inexpensive and you can plant lilies around your property to beautify your yard, as well as provide materials for a practical ritual tool.

Wand

The wand was sometimes called the "magic knife," but is best described as an apotropaic wand. Its primary function was to turn away evil, particularly evil spirits. Unlike the stick wand used in modern pagan practices, this wand was boomerang-shaped, with a curve like a crescent moon, and flat, like a throwstick. Flocks of wild birds symbolized the forces of chaos in Egyptian art, so the throwsticks used to kill or stun them could have symbolized the victory of order over chaos.[6] For the magician, this wand served as a tool and an emblem of control over devils and powerful spirits.

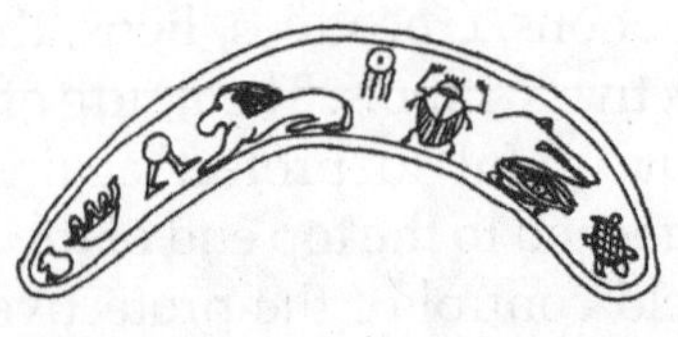

The wands of approximately 2800 B.C. were made of ivory and etched with early representations of supernatural and divine beings. Later, wands were elaborately carved with pictures of numerous creatures and inscriptions. One rounded end of the wand might have a jackal head carved on it, while the other end might contain a lion or a panther head. Bulls, lions, snakes, scarab-beetles, crocodiles, and supernatural creatures like the griffin and the double sphinx were among the many chosen guardians and symbols of protection carved onto the wands.

The creatures who appeared upon the wands were fighters, brandishing torches and knives, and depicted strangling or stabbing serpents and other menacing beasts. Two of the most popular figures were Taweret, the hippopotamus goddess, and Bes, an ugly, stubby-legged dwarf with the mane and ears of a lion.

Some wands were custom made for a particular magician, and included an inscribed formula that vowed to protect its user against all enemies and dangerous beings encountered in magical work. A typical inscription might read:

> Words spoken by these gods: We have come in order to protect the lady (or man) of the house, X.[7]

---

6 Geraldine Pinch, *Magic in Ancient Egypt*, p. 40.

7 Geraldine Pinch, *Magic in Ancient Egypt*, p. 42.

How to Make a Wand: To make this wand, you may use any type of wood, especially since ivory is undesirable and difficult to acquire. You will need a large square or rectangular piece of wood, a pencil, a jigsaw or band saw, a Dremel power tool or a chisel, gouge, and hammer for carving symbols and decorations, and some sand paper.

1. With a pencil, draw the boomerang shape of the wand onto the piece of wood. Size is entirely at your discretion. Choose a size that you can grasp comfortably in your hand.
2. Cut the shape of the wand with a jigsaw or a band saw. Be careful when using the power saw. Wear eye protection.
3. Sand the edges of the wand to a round, smooth finish. Next, sand its surface smooth.
4. You can carve or paint symbols and pictorials on the wand if you wish.

Use this wand during all evocations in your magical practice. Hold it in either hand and "throw" or whip it forward during an evocation to simulate the realistic throw of a throwstick. This gesture, coupled with your symbolic decorations and spell formulas, will ensure your success in conjuring unruly spirits.

Sistrum

Music played an important part in all temple rituals. One instrument used regularly was the sistrum, a kind of rattle that was sacred to the goddess Het-heru.[8] The sistrum was held by gods, pharaohs, priests, and priestesses. Priestesses held it in their right hand, and the menat (discussed below) in their left.[9]

---

[8] Barbara Watterson, *Gods of Ancient Egypt* (New York: Facts on File Publications, 1985), p. 127.

[9] E. A. Wallis Budge, *Egyptian Book of the Dead*, p. 245.

The sistrum was made of metal or faience.[10] It resembled a Het-heru head, with its horns bent around to form a loop. Threaded through three holes on each "horn" were three thin metal rods. Each rod passed across the loop from one side to the other. Metal beads were sometimes placed upon the rods, which were left loose in their sockets so that, when shaken, the sistrum rattled.

How to Make a Sistrum: You can make your own sistrum by using the description and illustration. To do so, you will need a number of items sold in plumbing and hardware stores: three thin metal rods, each about two inches longer than the distance between the matching holes of the sistrum (these can be copper or any metal, even a coat hanger); a two-foot length of flexible copper tubing about 1 inch in diameter to shape into a loop; a solid copper or brass pipe ten inches long and one inch in diameter.

You'll also need an adhesive for permanently joining metal piping together (ask the store clerk for his/her recommendation), some pliers, a power drill with a drill bit slightly larger in diameter than the three metal rods, a C-clamp or vise, a worktable, and some metal beads (to add more volume to the sound of the sistrum). Tell the hardware store clerk what you are making and ask for help in selecting your supplies. You may want to take along a picture of a sistrum.

1. Bend the tubing into a loop that can be permanently affixed in the handle. Measure, as evenly as possible, where the three holes need to be placed on each side of the loop so that the rods rest loosely and are parallel. Do not place the three holes on either side too close together. Mark the drill targets on the metal with a black magic marker or a dab of paint.
2. Lay the full length of copper tube on a worktable. Secure it to the table with a C-clamp or a vise.

---

[10] Barbara Watterson, *Gods of Ancient Egypt*, p. 127.

3. Drill the six holes completely through each marked target using a power drill and a drill bit slightly larger than the diameter of the metal rods. Be certain to have an experienced individual help you drill the holes safely. Have the tube properly secured as you drill. Do not hold the loop in one hand and drill with your other hand.
4. Bend the loop and push its ends into the opening of the copper pipe/handle. If required, pinch the ends of the loop together with pliers to squeeze it into the handle. The loop will stay inside the handle once firmly fitted, but it is a good idea to secure it with adhesive. Apply the adhesive generously inside the handle and on the loop ends. Allow it to dry for a day or two.
5. Place your metal rods into their holes as described above. With the pliers, bend each rod at a 90-degree angle on one end, and then pass the straight end through its first hole. If you wish to use metal beads, place them on the rod now.
6. Slide the straight end through its other hole. Use the pliers to bend the end of the rod to a 90-degree angle, in the opposite direction from the other end. Do the same for the other two rods.

You have successfully created the ancient sistrum.

Menat

The menat was an object presented to the gods with the sistrum. A host presented it to guests at a feast. Priestesses held it in their left hand, with the sistrum in their right, at religious festivals and certain temple rituals. These two instruments were emblems of the priestesses' office.

The menat is often called "the counterpoise of a collar." It consists of a disk with a handle attached and a cord.[11] It serves as a bead necklace with counterpoise to hang down the back of the wearer. The disk was made of faience, bronze, or hard stone, and was often inscribed with hieroglyphic words of power or adoration. The handle was usually made of bronze. It was worn around the neck, or carried in the left hand by its handle. As an amulet, it brought joy to its bearer. Used in temple ceremonies, it was believed to possess magical properties.

How to Make a Menat: The process of making a menat is unknown. We can speculate how to do so, however. Brass, copper, or bronze can be used as the handle. A circular piece of stone or bronze can serve as the disk. It may be a good idea to use bronze, copper, or brass for both the handle and the disk so they can be soldered together with a soldering gun for durability. In research, I found no instructions for attaching a stone disk to a bronze handle.

An assortment of colored or metal beads can be strung on strong necklace threads available at craft shops. The top of the handle will need to have two holes drilled in it, as discussed in the sistrum section above. The two holes should line up on either side of the handle top so that you can pass the necklace strand through the handle to secure it.

Keep in mind that the menat was worn around the neck. Do not make it too large or heavy if you intend to wear it in your ceremonies.

Figures

The Egyptians believed it was possible to transmit the spirit of a man, woman, child, god, or unworldly being into an inanimate figure or statue that then took on the qualities and attributes of that person or being. It was a common belief in Egypt that figures or statues possessed indwelling spirits of the people or beings they represented.

---

[11] E. A. Wallis Budge, *Egyptian Book of the Dead*, p. 245.

From Egypt, by way of Greece and Rome, the use of wax figures passed into Western Europe and England. In the Middle Ages it enjoyed great favor.[12] If a cult decided to take over a temple belonging to another god or goddess, they would shatter any figures or statues of the deity so that the deity's spirit would no longer have a place to dwell, and would become powerless. The cult would then replace the figures with representations of their deity who would thenceforth reside in the temple in spirit and rule in power.

Symbolic ceremonies and the recital of words of power over figures brought the desired spirit and its powers to dwell in a figure. The spirit could then be used for both good and evil at the will of the magician. Magicians used wax figures to obtain their desires and succeed over their enemies. They also made provisions for the happiness and well-being of the deceased by making Shabti figures of servants and laborers out of various materials to aid the dead in the underworld.

Magical figures were primarily made of wax. The wax was purchased or homemade. When a situation presented itself, a mass of wax was whittled and shaped to look like the person or creature it represented. It was not necessary that the wax figures be life-size or even perfect in design. Magical formulas were recited over the figure to send its spirit into the objective universe to do the magician's will.

A Spell Using a Wax Figure: There were many spells employing wax figures. One, for the purpose of ridding oneself of an enemy, specifies that the magician must be washed and ceremonially pure. He writes in green color upon a piece of new papyrus the names of the enemy(ies), as well as those of the enemy's father, mother, and children. He makes a wax

---

[12] E. A. Wallis Budge, *Egyptian Magic*, pp. 97, 98.

figure of the enemy and inscribes the enemy's name on the figure. The figure is tied with black hair and then cast upon the ground and kicked about with the left foot. Next, the magician pierces the figure with a stone spear head. Finally, the wax figure is cast into a fire. In chapter 6 you will learn magical spells that include the use of wax figures.

Aristotle's Use of Wax Figures: In the 13th century, an Arab writer, Abu-Shaker, wrote of the wax figures Aristotle had made from knowledge acquired of the Egyptian art. Aristotle gave Alexander the Great a box inside which several wax figures were nailed down. The box had a chain, so that Alexander could carry it wherever he traveled. Aristotle taught him how to recite magic words over the box whenever he set it down or picked it up. The box was not to leave Alexander's presence—even if it had to be specially carried by a servant.

The figures in Aristotle's box represented the armed forces that opposed Alexander. Some of the figures held leaden swords, curled backward, in their tiny hands. Others held spears that pointed to the ground, or bows with cut strings. All the figures were laid face down in the box. Aristotle had learned from Egyptian magic that such figures assured that any armies who challenged Alexander the Great would be powerless.

Statues as Magical Figures: The magical use of statues was similar to that of wax figures. Temples had shrines on their walls in which a statue of the temple deity was placed. Statues were also placed on the altar to receive offerings. The statues of gods, along with their hieroglyphic inscriptions, served as talismans.

Statues were commonly made of wooden cores, black granite, tinted ivory, hollow bronze, faience, red granite, and quartzite. Wooden statues that were stuccoed, gold-leafed, or painted on the wood surface were most popular.

Queen Dalukah's Use of Magic Statues: A legend found in *Les Prairies d'Or*[13] describes an undated event in ancient Egypt when the army of Pharaoh drowned in the Red Sea after a battle. The surviving women and slaves feared being attacked by the kings of Syria and by various western armies. They appointed a woman named Dalukah as their queen.

Dalukah was wise and adept at magic. Her first action was to surround Egypt with a wall that was guarded by men. Around the enclosure, she placed stone figures of crocodiles and other threatening animals. Dalukah also made figures of the Syrian, western, and nomad tribesmen, as well as of the beasts they rode upon. If an army came from any part of Syria or Arabia to attack Egypt, the queen recited words of power over the figures of the soldiers riding their beasts, and they immediately disappeared underground. The same fate befell the living creatures the figures represented.

Queen Dalukah reigned for thirty years, proving the power of her sorcery. She collected plants, animals, and minerals, and learned the secrets of the attracting or repelling powers of nature. These collected items, along with her magical figures, she placed in many great temples.

Pictures

The Egyptians drew and painted pictures depicting gods, divine beings, and all of life. Picture-writing graced the exterior of buildings, while pictures covered the interior of temples, royal structures, and tombs. Pictorials were also engraved into stone. When words of power were recited over a picture, the spirit(s) of the subjects in the picture were summoned to dwell within it and could be influenced to assist in magical aims.

---

[13] B. de Meynard and P. de Courteille, eds., *Les Prairies d'Or* (Paris, 1863), tome ii, p. 398f.

The magical papyri in which formulas survive that use magical pictures each have different words of power. The instructions for creating and charging magical pictures were quite varied. You can create your own pictures and the words of power to accompany them for magic.

Cippus of Heru—A Famous Picture: The most famous picture of Egyptian magic is the Cippus of Heru (otherwise known as the Metternichstele), which was found in 1828 at the construction site of a Franciscan monastery. Although the exact date of the stele is unknown, it is thought to have been produced between 378 B.C. to 360 B.C. The picture is a gigantic talisman engraved with magical gods and beings, and words of power. Every god, demon, animal, and reptile of importance is depicted upon it.

It is thought the Egyptians made and used many Cippus. A Cippus was placed in a conspicuous area of the home, courtyard, or any building to protect its inhabitants from hostile beings, both visible and invisible. Its power was believed to be unconquerable.

Using Pictures in Magic: You can fashion such a picture for your own needs. You can choose simply to draw Egyptian gods, creatures, and other beings onto papyrus, your lamp wick, or white paper. If stone carving appeals to you, try to make a Cippus. You do not need artistic expertise to design magical pictures. There was never a rule that all pictures had to appear in a certain way, or be perfect. Part of the mystery in Egyptian magic is that each depiction of the deities, people, and creatures was unique. Your art work should reflect how you know the deities and other creatures in your mind's eye.

If you choose to draw pictures on papyrus, use the writing ink described in this chapter and in chapter 3. In chapter 6, certain magical formulas provide instruction for using magic pictures.

Knot Magic

There are many uses of linen knots in magic. Sometimes knots were used to bind a person, situation, or creature. In this instance, untying the knots was as vital a stage in casting the magical spell as initially tying them. Knots were used to prevent something from happening until the desired time or to catch and bind harmful spirits for disposal or for the magician's use.

Knotted cords and any use of knots is associated with the god Anpu, who, through his role in mummification, rules both binding and wrapping. In Graeco-Egyptian papyri, the knots used in magic were indeed called Anpu threads. The red hair ribbons of the Seven Het-herus, the sevenfold form of the goddess Het-heru, were used to bind and gain control of dangerous spirits. The ribbons were also used in love spells. (You will learn of the Seven Het-herus later in this chapter.) In a Graeco-Egyptian papyrus, the magician ties 365 knots in black thread, saying each time, "Keep him who is bound."[14]

Use linen knots in your magic as described above. Chapters 5 and 6 have spells that include instructions for using knots.

Gold Rings

Gold rings were used, especially in love spells. I have not included the original instructions for their use in this chapter, or later in chapter 6, because some ingredients that are not practical—such as the heart and gall of a shrew-mouse—are required.

In one formula, the embalmed tail of the shrew-mouse is pounded with myrrh and placed inside a gold ring. How this feat was accomplished is not known. After placing the ring onto a finger and reciting charms over it, any individual that the magician touched with the hand submitted to his/her desires. Another formula

---

[14] Geraldine Pinch, *Magic in Ancient Egypt*, p. 83.

called for the heart of a shrew-mouse to be set within a seal-ring of gold. Such a ring was believed to bring favor, love, and reverence. Seal-rings were engraved with a picture and served as amulets. Not all had animal organs inserted. You will learn how to use these rings in chapter 3.

Water

The Egyptians sprinkled the floor with water for the reception of visitors in the home, or when opening ceremonies in the temple. Water was recognized for its cleansing properties and was used to purify. Ancient Egyptians also visited buildings inside the district of a temple to drink or bathe in consecrated, holy water for healing. The water would also procure healing or prophetic dreams. Both uses can easily be incorporated into your magical practice.

Oil

In magic, different oils were used to achieve particular magical aims. From *The Leyden Papyrus* we learn of the following uses:

- To conjure a damned spirit to do your bidding, take an old wick and place clean butter in your lamp to burn during the conjuring. (The Egyptians used butter as an oil in this example.)
- To work love magic, place rose oil onto a clean wick and burn it in your lamp. Recite chosen words of power to charge it. (For love magic spells, see chapter 6.)
- Cedar oil was often used to anoint the forehead before working magic, and in some instances, during religious rituals.

Also from *The Leyden Papyrus,* the following blessing of oil is recited before using it. It is appropriate for healing and other forms of magic:

> Thou being praised, I will praise thee, O oil, I will praise thee, thou being praised by the Agathodaemon; thou being applauded by me myself, I will praise thee forever, O herb-oil—otherwise true oil—O sweat of the Agathodaemon, amulet of Seb. It is Auset who makes invocation to the oil. O true oil, O drop of rain, O water-drawing of the planet Jupiter which cometh down from the sun-boat at dawn.

The Agathodaemon is an almighty four-faced daemon—the highest darkling in Egyptian mythology.[15] This is not to suggest that the oil used in Egyptian magic was evil or negative. It simply means that oil contained great power for use in whatever way the magician chose.

Herbs and Minerals

Herbs were used particularly in healing magic. The problem of defining what herbs and minerals were frequently used and how they were used, has been a struggle for even the most scholarly Egyptologist.

The Egyptians had their own names for plants and minerals. Translators of papyri have been able to identify some of these, but generally list them as vocabulary with little notation on how each was used.

Herbs: Chamomile, paeonia, rush-leaf, saffron, rue, houseleek, plants of the fennel family, wild garlic, and pepper were used in medicine. The use of herbs in Egypt was probably similar to their use in the herbal medicine of today.

Herbs and plants were also used to fashion wreaths, which were sold by wreath sellers and made by magicians to project magical properties. Mention of wreaths placed upon altars at funeral ceremonies can be found in *The Egyptian Book of the Dead*. There is also brief

---

[15] F. L. Griffith and Herbert Thompson, eds., *The Leyden Papyrus*, Col. IV, 1.17.

mention in magical papyri that wreaths were placed on shrines and altars during certain temple ceremonies.

Saffron is a plant with purplish flowers and orange stigmas that yielded orange-yellow dye and seasoning from its dried stigmas. It served as a dye for clothing, and possibly as a writing ink.

Minerals: Many magnetic minerals were used in medicine and magic. Magnetic iron ore and *magnes mas* are two magnetic minerals frequently used. It is assumed that the Egyptians harnessed the magnetic forces of the Earth by employing such minerals in magic.

Native sulfur and other minerals were sometimes mixed together with herbs to alleviate the pain of gout.

Natron is a mineral of hydrous sodium-carbonate, which was used for embalming the dead and in some magic formulas. It was heated with other salts and spices, then mixed with honey for embalming.

Salt was not often used in spells, which is interesting, since it played such a crucial role in Egyptian life, agriculture, and death. Chapter 5 includes a sample divination setup in which lumps of salt are employed. This is the only formula of its kind found in my research.

Altar

Elegant altars, decorated with plants, lotus flowers, liberation vases, haunches of beef, fish, loaves of bread and cakes, vases of wine and oil, containers holding beer and wax, a wreath, fruits, and various cut flowers, were used during funeral ceremonies and in temples. While elaborate altars were not used in divination, they were used during certain religious and magical rites.

Altars served as places to present offerings to the deities. At the close of rituals or magical rites, the perishable food items were eaten by the priesthood. This was not a formal ceremony in itself, but rather a time of casual and social dining.

Storage of Implements

Magical implements were often stored in special boxes. The great priestly official, the *kher heb,* was so much in the habit of performing acts of magic that he kept a box of materials and instruments always ready for the purpose.[16]

During the l 9th Dynasty, it became popular for priesthood members to store their magic utensils in niches in the wall. These niches could be in the magician's private study, where he wrote and conducted magic spells, or within a temple. The east wall is commonly specified in papyri as the place to build such a niche. Once the niche was built, it also acted as a wall altar. The magician either removed materials to conduct divination or magic elsewhere, or worked at the niche itself, using it as an altar.

You can place your journals, magical tools, and other materials into similar storage areas. Certainly, the first is the most practical.

[16] E. A. Wallis Budge, *Egyptian Magic,* p. 70.

Chapter Three

Amulets

em sa-k user-tu ma neteru
Thy protector, being powerful with the gods.

The use of amulets has existed since the beginning of humanity, and continues. Amulets represent beliefs and superstitions so old that even the Egyptians were, at times, doubtful about their origin and meaning.[1]

Amulets are perhaps the most renowned artifacts of ancient Egypt. They were used in Egypt long before literacy prevailed. The word *amulet* is taken from an Arabic root which means "to bear, to carry." It defines a broad class of objects and adornments that were made of various materials employed to protect or otherwise serve the individual. They were used by both the living and the dead to protect from visible and invisible enemies. Charged with words of power, amulets radiated supernatural powers that all classes of Egypt considered necessary to life.

Amulet Types

There are two types of Egyptian amulets: those inscribed with magical script and those that were not inscribed.

[1] E. A. Wallis Budge, *Egyptian Magic* (New York: Dover, 1971), p. 26.

Prayers or magical words were recited over amulets worn by the living and also placed on the dead at funeral ceremonies. The common man did not have the power to employ them. Only magicians and priests held the power to charge amulets for use. The process included carving the words of power upon the objects, which then were believed to have a threefold power: the power inherent in the substance of which the amulet was made, the power of the words recited over them, and the power that lay in the words inscribed.

Amulets were crafted of gods in human or creature form. These were placed on jewelry, headrests, temples, and every conceivable furnishing or object. Bangle bracelets often served as amulets. Selections of hieroglyphic signs and pictorials decorated the bangles, which were commonly made in silver and gold. Hieroglyphic signs like the *wedjat*, *ankh*, and *djed* pillars were used. Snakes, baboons, falcons, turtles, and the horned mask of the goddess Bat are also among the many pictures used.

Old seals from jars, boxes, and documents were considered powerful amulets. Those inscribed with royal titles or the Pharaoh's throne names were sought after for their immense power and value. Certain seals were strung on cords and worn like beads.

Amulet Uses

In the magical papyri, we learn that the magicians placed great importance on how amulets were worn. There were three primary ways of wearing amulets: as pendants worn around the neck, as bracelets, and as amulet bags.

Pendants were worn for the protection or empowerment the wearer derived from them. They were also used to express the devotion a person had to a particular deity. These pendants allowed the wearer to use the divine image and power of a god or goddess to accomplish goals in daily life, and in magic. They depicted animals, plants, deities, tools, furniture, ritual objects, and parts of the human body. They were made out of stone and many other natural materials. Typically, pendants were carved, engraved, or drawn upon to capture a form that would give power. A good example of this is the scarab, which was a popular amulet of Egypt made of the genuine scarab beetle, or of an imitation carved from many types of stones.

Written magic, or small magical objects, were later placed within cylindrical pendants made of gold, silver, and other materials. These could be opened and closed. Amulet bags also held magical script written on papyrus or linen. These bags were tied around the neck or worn elsewhere on the body. Children wore amulet bags that contained divine decrees issued in the name of the god or goddess who gave an oracle as to the child's fate in life. The oracle was written on papyrus or linen and then rolled up and placed in the amulet case or bag to be worn. The decrees commonly were positive, assuring that the child would live a long, healthy, and prosperous life. Some decrees vowed to protect against sorcerers, the Evil Eye, and numerous hazards. Others promised to help the owner of the amulet cheat fate.

Amulet bags were popular. *Sa* is an Egyptian word that can mean a group of objects, the cord they were strung on, the bag that contained them, or the words and gestures needed to "activate" them.[2] A looped cord is the hieroglyph used to write this word. The cord itself was made of leather or linen thread, and served as an amulet in its own right. Many were tied with several knots by the magician in the course of a rite.

---

[2] Geraldine Pinch, *Magic in Ancient Egypt* (Austin, TX: University of Texas Press, 1995), p. 108.

Amulets were worn by children to fight off disease and injuries like the sting of a scorpion. Women wore them to protect against risks in childbirth. A pregnant woman often wore one or two amulet bags containing an assortment of ingredients to protect her during childbirth. The contents might have included parts of the lip and ear of a donkey, a dried chameleon, the head of a hoopoe, seven silk threads (representing the Seven Het-herus), or a written magical spell. If a woman battled infertility, an amulet made from any object that resembled the male or female genitals, or a pregnant woman, was a powerful aid. Women and children also wore amuletic bracelets, earrings, and anklets.

Quarrying expeditions, hunting, traveling by sea, and warfare were common hazards for men. Amulets, as well as magical spells, served as practical protection for these activities. Amuletic belt clasps were worn below the navel by men. As Egyptians believed a person's emotions and power resided in the stomach, these clasps were probably used to protect or empower that region. Men also wore amuletic bracelets. In 1700 B.C., rings became popular.

Dreams fell under the protection of amulets. Headrests were constructed of limestone and engraved with the god Bes grasping and biting snakes that represented the dangers of the night, among which were dreams. Each period of sleep was believed to be a brief excursion into the underworld, where spirits and demons could cause nightmares. While dreams were thought useful in divination, they also threatened intrusion by unsavory, unworldly beings into the life of the sleeper. This may provide another clue as to why permanent amulets existed that could be used around the clock.

Some amulets were worn permanently, usually in the form of jewelry. Others were used in temporary situations that required the immediate influence of a charged aid, such as illness, injury, or childbirth. These magical objects were made and used in countless ways. Surviving amulets exhumed and studied by Egyptologists have given us a great deal of knowledge about them. In chapters 5 and 6, you will learn how to use amulets in divination and magic.

Amulet Deities

In magical papyri of the second millennium B.C., the goddesses Auset and Nebt-het are associated with spinning and weaving linen cords to make amulets, especially amulets of health. Another deity named Hedjhotep, is similarly depicted. The goddess Neith accepts the woven cords from these gods and goddesses, and ties knots in them for magic. Pictures of the deities associated with making amulets were often drawn on linen and served as temporary amulets.

Materials Used to Make Amulets

Because amulets were traded, exported, and copied throughout the ancient world, countless examples have survived. The earliest Egyptian amulets were made of green schist, which was cut into various shapes of animals and creatures. Numerous samples were found in the prehistoric graves of Egypt. Archaeologists found amulets that had served as spiritual and magical offerings in houses, temples, and shrines.

In later times, carnelian, green basalt, gold, granite, marble, blue paste, blue and red glass, glazed porcelain, red jasper, obsidian, hematite, lapis lazuli, bronze, wood, and numerous other substances were used in the manufacture of amulets. The Egyptians used such a variety of natural stones in their design that you can probably make an amulet today of just about any type of stone and remain within tradition.

Natural or man-made objects can serve as the raw materials for amulets. The material, shape, scarcity, texture, or color of a natural substance can be the source of its power. Strange and rare materials were thought to hold the most power. Seashells and river pebbles were commonly used. Plants and long-lasting herbs were used, although few such amulets have survived. Cowrie shells shaped like an eye or the female genitals were used as amulets popular for warding off the Evil Eye. Girdles were made from cowries to protect a woman's fertility. Imitation cowries were made in gold, silver, and faience.

Other natural amulets include animal parts like claws, cat hair, a snake's fang, a camel's tooth, and various other portions of animal bodies. Many, such as the head of a hoopoe, are impractical and undesirable today.

How Egyptians Charged Amulets

Any object that can be worn or carried, and is charged in a ceremonial rite with energy through inscription or spoken magical script, can serve as an amulet. The power of an amulet is made possible by the magician infusing it with energy and inscribing upon it or reciting to it some purpose that will serve its owner. The charged amulet will amplify that energy and promote its purpose. In Egypt, magicians were summoned by royalty and laymen who required the special quality of an amulet to overcome a situation, gain protection, or to be empowered in some fashion. Commoners also made and used their own amulets. If an individual had an object to infuse with the needed power and had some way of charging it, it became a functioning amulet.

How to Make an Amulet Using Modeling Compound: Modeling compound is perhaps the best choice for making amulet pendants, since it is easy to use. You will need a pencil, one sheet of paper, modeling compound (which you can purchase at a craft shop), a piece of craft wire approximately two inches long, two sheets of waxed paper, a small knife, a standard oven, some acrylic paints, and a small paint brush.

1. Choose the shape for your amulet and draw it onto a piece of paper. This will serve as a pattern.
2. Roll out and flatten a three-inch ball of the compound between two pieces of waxed paper.
3. With a small knife, cut out the shape and details of your amulet in the compound, using your pattern.
4. Place a loop of craft wire through the top.
5. Bake the amulet in your oven following the manufacturer's instructions.
6. Once baked, use the acrylic paints to decorate your amulet.

Place your completed amulet on a leather throng or gold chain to wear it. Wood is also ideal for making amulets. You can carve a picture of the amulet shape onto a wood surface, or carve the amuletic object from the wood. Stone and metals require a specialized skill in cutting and design. Amulets were also written on linen, papyrus, thin sheets of metal, and the leaves of certain plants. You can choose to employ written and drawn amulets instead of carving or engraving figures. Write down the magical script or drawing of your choice, roll it up, and wear it around your neck as an amulet.

You can wear your written magic by inserting it into a pill box and some small vessel pendants. Vessel pendants are used to hold essential oils, perfume, and a variety of substances. These can be purchased at most jewelry stores. These modern vessels are very similar to the Egyptian cylindrical pendants.

How to Charge an Amulet: You are provided with a list of Egyptian amulets in the next section. These can be used for several purposes. First, you need to know how to charge an amulet to capture its power. The example

Figure 9. Vulture amulet.

below is typical of how an ancient magician charged an amulet. You may follow these instructions for any amulet listed below. I will use the amulet of the vulture in the following example. The amulet of the vulture was intended to bring the power of Auset, known as "the Divine Mother." Traditionally, it was made of gold in the form of a hovering vulture, with the sign of infinity, the *shen*, held in each talon. (See figure 9.)

1. You can choose to simply draw the vulture onto a piece of papyrus or white paper. You can also take a small piece of wood or stone that can be worn around the neck and carve this amulet upon its surface. Any material, natural or man-made, is suitable for use.
2. Once you have made your amulet, you need to charge it with words of power before wearing it. You may conduct this ritual in as ceremonial a way as desired.

3. Choose a private location or room in your home where you can conduct the charging without interruption.
4. You may wish to decorate an altar for charging the amulet. Lit incense, consecrated water, anointing oil, and other items help to shift your consciousness and enhance the environment for your ritual. Lay the vulture amulet in the center of your altar, surrounded by the above purifying items.
5. The following magical script is taken from chapter 157 of *The Book of the Dead*, but we know that the living also used this amulet. (I was unable to find appropriate magical script to charge it for this purpose.)

The script begins by describing the care Auset provided Heru when she raised him in the papyrus swamps. Next, it tells of Heru's acceptance into the company of gods. It ends with a description of Heru's war with Set, whom he conquered through the power and protection of his mother, Auset. By reciting this script over your amulet, you charge it with the power of Auset and of Heru. You will be made victorious. Battles can be won. You are protected under Auset, the mighty goddess of magic.

> Auset cometh and hovereth over the city, and she goeth about seeking the secret habitations of Heru as he emergeth from his papyrus swamps, and she raiseth up his shoulder which is in evil case. He is made one of the company in the divine boat, and the sovereignty of the whole world is decreed for him. He hath warred mightily, and he maketh his deeds to be remembered; he hath made the fear of him to exist and awe of him to have its being. His mother, the mighty lady, protecteth him, and she hath transferred her power unto him.

When the charge is complete, you may wish to anoint your amulet with a dab of water or oil to consecrate it and "seal" the charge.

Using Your Amulets

Amulets can serve a variety of your needs. They can protect you from fierce entities conjured through evocation or negative energies released during magical ceremonies. Traveling a long distance from home, taking an unnerving test, fighting an illness, or decreasing the effects of an enemy's work against you are only a few of the situations in which an amulet can provide protection, or empowerment. Amulets can serve you well at any time in your life that you feel vulnerable or feel the need to have your power protected or charged.

Egyptian Amulets

This section provides the most popular amulets used in divination and magic by the living. It lists the amulet name, illustration, definition, and how the amulet can be used.

Ankh

The ankh is perhaps the most popular amulet to survive to our modern day. They are found in most jewelry stores and are worn traditionally around the neck, just as they were in Egypt. Typically, they are made of gold, sterling silver, copper, and many other metals.

The ankh is a symbol of life that is thousands of years old. As an amulet, it is used to lengthen and protect life. In Egypt's earliest history, the ankh existed as a popular amulet that every god carried. As a hieroglyphic sign, ankh is the word for life. Its exact origin, or what the ankh represents in form, is hotly debated. Some Egyptologists claim that it represents a penis sheath, while others state that it is the form of a sandal strap, since in ancient Egypt, this strap had a name which resembled the word for life.

Because the ankh is also a hieroglyphic sign, its power can be captured simply by writing it. This can be done during any magical work, or it can be drawn on papyrus, rolled up, and worn on a cord. The ankh is often seen on ancient jewelry with the wedjat and the djed pillar. Combined, these three symbols provide potent protection.

Animals are also found on artifacts with the ankh, among them snakes, baboons, turtles, and falcons. It is logical to choose fierce and intelligent animals to place beside the ankh. These, and the two additional symbols above, were often fashioned into gold and silver necklaces to be worn by a child.

It is interesting to note the apparent relationship between the Egyptian word *akh,* which describes the part of a deceased person that acquired magical powers in the afterlife,[3] and that of the ankh as a word and amulet.

Buckle (Tyet)

The buckle or *tyet* is symbolic of the girdle of Auset. It is typically made of gold, gold-plated metals, wood, black stone, red glass, red jasper, carnelian, and other red substances. The color red is symbolic of the blood of Auset. The tyet was worn as a pendant.

This amulet comes from a story in Egyptian mythology. When Set killed his brother, Ausar, he did not know that Ausar's consort, Auset was pregnant and carrying Ausar's heir, Heru. Terrified that Set would find out she was pregnant and kill her, Auset fled to Chemmis in the Delta, where she gave birth to Heru. To protect the newborn Heru, she took off her girdle and tied it around him. It is the knot of this magic girdle that was used to form the amulet tyet, which became a symbol of protection to

3 Geraldine Pinch, *Magic in Ancient Egypt,* p. 179.

the Egyptians.[4] The tyet also gives power to access every place in the underworld and allows the wearer to point "one hand toward heaven, and one hand toward earth." This makes it a powerful ally in evocation, out of body projection, or any magical work.

You can make the tyet amulet out of any material. Red-colored stone or other material is best. To charge the amulet and obtain the power of Auset's blood, recite the following secret script over it:

> The blood of Auset, and the strength of Auset, and the words of power of Auset shall be mighty to act as powers to protect this great and divine being, and to guard him (or her) from him that would do unto him anything that he holdeth in abomination.

String the amulet on a pith cord and wear it around your neck for protection and empowerment.

Frog

The frog is a symbol of the birth goddess, Heqet, who appears as a human woman with a frog's head and typical Egyptian wig. Heqet is a primordial creator-goddess. Because Heqet helped Ausar rise from the dead after Set murdered him, the frog is also a symbol of resurrection.

Frogs appeared on gold rings around 1400 B.C. These rings sometimes had a frog depicted on one side of the bezel and a scorpion, representing the protective goddess Serqet, on the other. It is thought that these rings were worn as protective amulets in life and by women in childbirth.

Frogs also appeared on glazed steatite magic rods around 1800–1700 B.C. For a magician to place this symbol upon such a vital ritual tool signifies that it had great

4 Barbara Watterson, *Gods of Ancient Egypt* (New York: Facts on File Publications, 1985), p. 93.

importance, probably as a puissant amulet of creation. Small amulet pendants of frogs have been found in burial chambers. These amulets, made from alabaster, carnelian, and other natural materials, were part of funeral ceremonies promising resurrection.

You can make a frog amulet out of wood or inscribe its form onto a stone for a necklace. If drawn onto candles, papyrus, paper, and magical tools, the shape serves to amplify your magical creations. For a woman, this amulet has a particular meaning. The women of Egypt swore by its ability to protect during the phases of a woman's cycles, life, and childbirth. It was thus worn with special pride by women, symbolizing their role in the creation of life and existence.

Lion

The fierce disposition and strength of the lion made it popular for protective amulets. The Egyptians believed that two lions guarded the eastern and western horizons. The Lion of the Eastern Horizon observed the rising Sun each morning, and the Lion of the Western Horizon guarded the Sun by night. Lions lived in the deserts, and the Egyptians reasoned that the Sun died there each evening, then was born again there in the morning.

Egyptians required a guardian at night so that a new day of living could be experienced each morning. Beds and headrests were decorated with lion motifs. A lion made of faience was threaded onto red linen and secured to a man's hand as a protective amulet during sleep, to guard against all visible and invisible life-forms that could cause nightmares, health problems, and threaten harm.

Images of lions decorated jewelry and magical tools. Lion amulets were used symbolically in magic to defend against chaotic entities, negative energies, and hostile deities. Enemies were easily trampled under foot as the lion, along with other dangerous animals, worked to defend the magician.

Lotus Flower

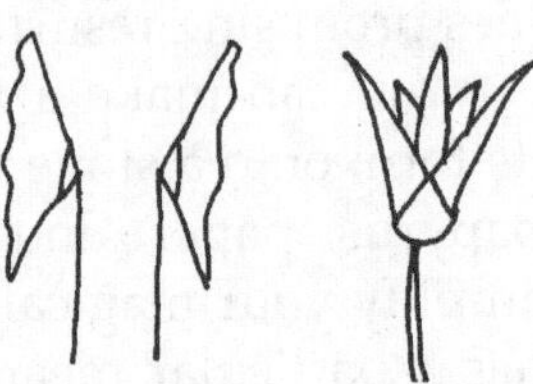

To the Egyptians, the white and blue lotuses were the perfect flowers. The blue lotus was sacred because its delightful perfume was the divine essence and sweat of the Sun god, Ra. The lotus adorned columns inside temples and on the porticos which led to courtyards at the villas of the wealthy. It was revered as a symbol of regeneration: The lotus rises from the water each dawn to open its petals to the Sun god, Ra.[5]

Goddesses and priestesses are portrayed carrying the lotus/lily wand in statues, in paintings upon tomb walls, and in papyri which depict religious and magical ceremonies. Women carried real lotus flowers for pleasure and in religious rituals. This symbol of regeneration can be used in magical spells prompting a new beginning, upon love charms, in spiritual ceremony, and for any situation requiring reformation.

Menat

The might of the male and female organs ofgeneration are supposed to be mystically united within the menat,[6] which represents the power of the primordial reproduction that began all life. This amulet was used in Egypt as early as the 6th Dynasty. Gods, kings, priests, and priestesses wore or carried the menat. It can be worn around the

---

5 Time-Life Books Editors, *TimeFrame 3000–1500 BC: The Age of God-Kings* (Alexandria, VA: Time-Life Books, 1987), p. 71.

6 E. A. Wallis Budge, *Egyptian Magic*, p. 61.

neck or carried in the hand. It is believed to possess magical properties and to bring health, joy, and strength to its owner.

The menat was held in the left hand by priestesses at religious festivals and offered to the gods at shrines within homes and temples. In the home, it was also presented to guests by their hosts as a sign of hospitality. The menat was the ideal gift to wish good tidings to another person.

The goddess Het-heru is associated with the menat. She represents love, beauty, and happiness, and was sometimes invoked by the Egyptians to nurse the sick and depressed. The root word for nurse is related to the word menat, which further enforces its use as a word of power to soothe emotions and bring well-being to its owner.

Menat pendants and hand-held devices found in Egypt often have inscriptions to Het-heru upon the disk. One such inscription reads, "Beloved of Het-heru, lady of sycamore trees." Such written magic was used to charge the amulet, and to harness Het-heru's power and derive the sacredness of the sycamore tree.

The menat is a curious object. It consists of a disk with an attached handle and a cord. Pendants were made of faience and hard stone. The hand-held version often had a handle and disk made of bronze. The disk was hollow and bore inscriptions like the head of a cow, which is the sacred animal to Het-heru.

Chapter 2 gives further information on how to make a hand-held menat to use in your practice.

Nefer

The *nefer* was a musical instrument that was played in Egypt. For the Pharaoh's amusement, musicians, dancers, and acrobats often performed before royalty within the great hall. Beautifully adorned ladies wearing cones of scented fat atop their heads strummed the nefer, as dancers glided to its sound. This instrument may also have been used in temple ceremonies. Similar to our modern guitar, its strings were plucked with the fingers.

The amulet represents the cheerful sound of the actual instrument, which brought feelings of good fortune and happiness. It was made small enough to wear as a pendant, and carved from red stone, carnelian, red porcelain, and other substances. It was a favorite pendant, often worn attached to necklaces and strings of beads.

You can make a nefer by carving its shape into stone or wood. You can also draw it on papyrus or paper, or carve it from candle wax. Use it in magic for good fortune, to obtain favor, and to ensure success.

Papyrus Scepter

This amulet represented the scepter used by priests, priestesses, royalty, and the gods in both religious and magical ceremonies. The scepter is also symbolic of power and authority.

In early Egypt, the amulet apparently was used only in funeral ceremonies. In the 24th Dynasty and beyond, it seems that it represented the power of Auset, who derived her own power from her father, the husband of Renenutet, the goddess of abundant harvests and food.[7] Traditionally, it was made from light-green or blue porcelain, or mother-of-emerald, and was worn on a cord.

You may design your own scepter out of any material to wear or carry with you. You can draw the scepter onto papyrus, roll it up, and place it inside a vessel-pendant to wear around your neck.

The papyrus scepter is best used in magic for vigor, renewal, and to harvest needed things. Healing magic,

---

7 E. A. Wallis Budge, *Egyptian Magic*, p. 49.

success, and good fortune are possible uses, and it may be used to harvest the love of another in love spells.

Scarab

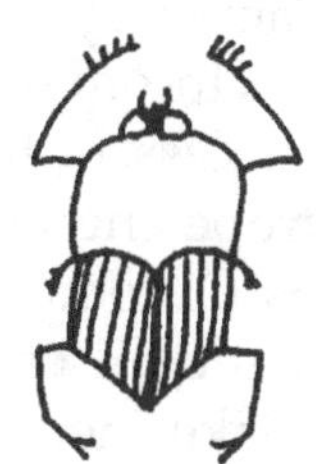

The scarab is the best known of Egyptian amulets. The scarab beetle is a dung beetle that rolls a ball of dung with its hind legs, lays its eggs in it, and then buries it in a dug hole. The scarab beetle still exists today.

The scarab appealed to the Egyptians for its crafty wisdom in rolling dung and using it to lay its eggs in—both acts of creation. These beetles roll the balls from east to west, bury them for eight to twenty days, then fetch the balls and throw them in water so that the scarabaei can emerge. This process seemed to mimic the Sun as it was propelled across the sky. The Sun contained the germs of all life, and the insect's ball contained the germs of the young scarabs. Both were creatures who produced life in a special way.

The scarab-beetle amulet is an image of the god of becoming, Khepri, who is the regenerated Sun at dawn. It is symbolic of the continuous process of creation. The actual beetle was also used in magic, however. Magicians drowned the beetles in the milk of a black cow, then placed them on a brazier so that the gods summoned for divination would come quickly and answer inquiries truthfully. In early Egypt, if a magician wished to defeat some sorcery worked against him, he cut off the head and wings of a large scarab beetle, boiled them, steeped them in the oil of a serpent, and then drank the mixture.

Egyptians made scarab amulets by the thousands, and in numerous varieties. The amulet's common appeal did not diminish its power, however. It remained a potent amulet into the fourth century A.D. Amuletic bracelets were made of knotted leather cords, scarabs, snakes, and other amulet devices. These were used in divination to protect the magician, or his medium, from hostile gods and forces. In magic, it worked in much the same way.

In order for the amulet to work for gaining favor and success, or for use in love spells, it had to be made of heliotrope engraved with a scarab encircled by a snake known as Ouroboros—a snake swallowing its tail. This snake is symbolic of totality. The magical names of the scarab and snake should be written in hieroglyphs on the reverse side of the stone.

Scarab amulets were made of every kind of natural stone and metal. Green glazed scarab pendants were worn on a gold chain. Sometimes scarab amulets were made with a band of gold across and down the back where the wings joined together.

This amulet can be made from any substance. You can also buy scarab jewelry from sources found in the Egyptian Resources section. Words of power that charge it for magic are usually stamped or engraved around the scarab form.

How to Make a Scarab Ring: The spell below is similar to one found in *A Fragment of a Graeco-Egyptian Work upon Magic* (Publications of the Cambridge Antiquarian Society, 1852).[8] You can use this spell to charge any scarab amulet. To make a ring, you will need an oval of emerald or other green stone, a Dremel power tool and bits for stone engraving or other stone carving tools, thick gold wire that you can shape to the diameter of your finger.

1. Engrave the picture of a scarab onto the emerald stone. You can cut the form of the scarab into the stone, but it is difficult.
2. On the reverse side of the beetle, carve the figure of Auset.

---

8 E. A. Wallis Budge, *Egyptian Magic*, pp. 42–53.

3. Bore a channel through the stone and pass a gold wire through it.

You can conduct the following charge on the 7th, 9th, 10th, 12th, 14th, 16th, 21st, 24th, and 25th days of any month. To do so, you will need a scarab amulet, a table or altar, a small container or vessel, a square of linen cloth, a piece of olive wood (optional), a censer, myrrh and kyphi resin incense, chrysolite (see glossary), and an ointment of lilies, or myrrh, or cinnamon.

1. Place the amulet on a table. Lay a pure linen cloth and some olive wood under the table.
2. Set a small censer burning myrrh and kyphi in the center of the table as an offering.
3. Have a small vessel containing chrysolite in which you put ointment of lilies, or myrrh, or cinnamon.
4. Bless the scarab ring, then lay it in the vessel of ointment.
5. Offer it in the incense smoke from the censer.
6. Leave the ring in the ointment vessel for three days.
7. After three days, place some pure loaves, fruits of the season, vine sticks, and other offerings on the table.
8. Remove the scarab ring from the ointment and anoint yourself with it.

Anoint yourself early in the morning, facing east, and recite the following script:

> I am Tehuti, the inventor and founder of medicines and letters; come to me, thou that art under the earth, rise up to me, thou great spirit.

At dawn, it was believed that the Sun was under the Earth, and slowly emerging. In this magical script, you are summoning the powers of the god Khepri, the Sun, and charging your amulet permanently to use as you desire.

Scorpion

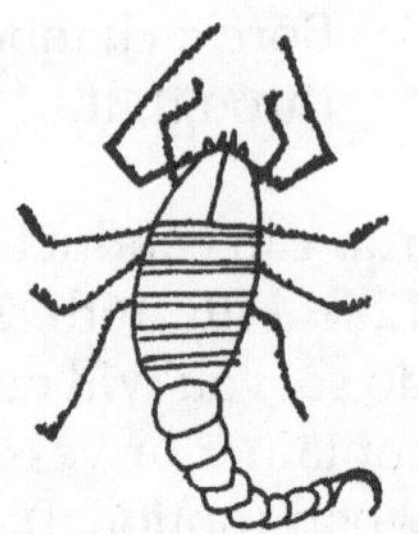

The scorpion symbolized chaos and was thought to have been the form taken by the restless dead. Scorpions posed an everyday threat as well. Its sting, aside from representing malicious ghosts, or amplifying the effects of the war between order and chaos, could prove deadly. Thus magicians used scorpion amulets to protect from the danger of hostile entities or the forces of chaos.

Scorpion amulets may have represented the goddess Serqet, who was depicted as a woman with a scorpion on her head. Serqet was considered a friendly goddess who helped at the birth of pharaohs and gods. She is also one of four goddesses who guarded embalmed bodies in funeral ceremonies. Serqet means "she who causes to breathe"—a name given to induce flattery so that her powers could be used against actual scorpion stings. The idea was to conquer the living scorpions with the identical power of their goddess. Serqet was used to heal, but she could also inflict harm on enemies.

Scorpion amulets were frequently used in medical magic and were placed around the neck of patients who had been stung, while words of power were spoken. They repelled peril and gave protection. A scorpion was often incised on the base of rings that had frog bezels. These rings were worn by children to protect them against scorpion stings. Another amulet used in a similar fashion was that of a serpent's head.

The Egyptians desired order and the well-being of all. Spells invoking the protection of the scorpion were placed on temple gateways, on plaques in houses, and on amulets. Scorpion pendants were made of many substances. Blue glass was a popular choice in the third through first centuries B.C., and some had traces of gilding.

You can make your amulet from wood, draw it upon papyrus, or cut its shape in a variety of stones.

The Number Seven

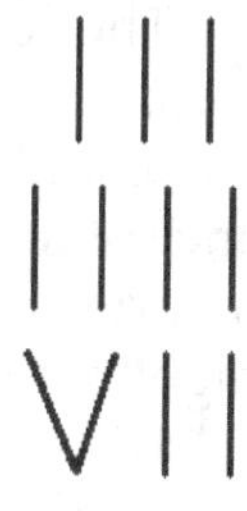

Seven was a number of great significance in Egyptian magic.[9] The goddesses Sekhmet and Het-heru both had seven forms. The actual number seven was not used on amulets, talismans, or for magic. Rather, the number's power was invoked by grouping deities, figures, statues, pictures, magical names, or just about anything in series or arrangements of seven.

The sevenfold Het-heru is a gentle, lovely sky goddess who delivered happiness and protected women and children. Her aspect of the Seven Het-herus partakes of the nature of good fairies.[10] Invoking the Seven Het-herus in divination and magic promised powerful assistance. They decreed fate, both good and bad. They were frequently invoked in love spells, one of which you will learn in chapter 6. They also declared the fate of newborn children.

Because magicians wished to avoid, or control, the effects of fate, ancient papyri tell us that they often had to work against the Seven Het-herus in order to acquire a desired outcome. If flattery and offerings did not succeed in convincing the Seven Het-herus, magicians employed negotiation, threats, or shape-shifted to a dominant god-form to achieve ultimate control of fate.

Sekhmet was created as the opposite form of Het-heru. She is the goddess of the burning Sun, war, destroyer of enemies, personification of the awesome power of the solar eye energy (see Eye of Ra, below). She was often invoked in magical rituals to protect the state of

---

9 Geraldine Pinch, *Magic in Ancient Egypt*, p. 37.

10 E. A. Wallis Budge, *Egyptian Book of the Dead* (New York: Dover, 1967), p. cxix.

Egypt. Ancient papyri state that the priests of Sekhmet seemed to specialize in medicine, and so her power could apparently be channeled for healing.

The Seven Arrows of Sekhmet guarantee misfortune, illness, or other negative effects. They were powerful weapons that could be harnessed by magicians for use in spells. One ancient spell uses them against the Evil Eye. Sekhmet also had seven negative messengers that could be sent to cause nightmares, illness, and numerous hazards to enemies.

Divination scripts included the invocation of seven kings, the Seven Het-herus, seven forms of Heru, and a score of entities in groups of seven. There are divine manifestations of messengers in groups of seven that were emanations of any deity, which were summoned for use in divination and magic.

In many divination scripts, scribes instructed that the script be recited seven times. The number seven retained importance in spoken magic. References to "seven heavens" and "seven sanctuaries" can also be found in numerous papyri.

You can use a sevenfold form of any deity in your practice. It seems that usually these were invoked or summoned through written magic. Making wax figures or statues in groups of seven for magical purposes invokes the number's power. Grouping the celestial heavens, and any spiritual or magical place or thing, by seven ensures great achievement.

Serpents

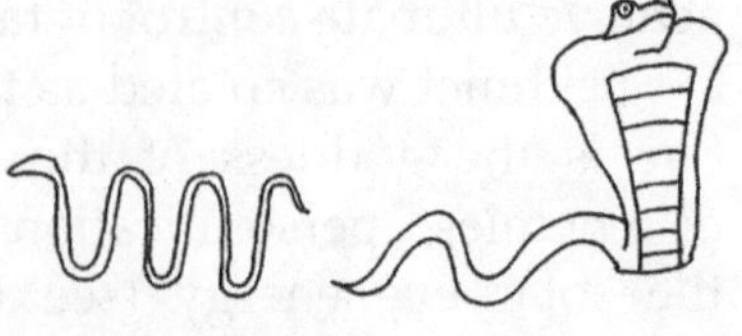

Serpents in many forms graced Egyptian amulets. Many were for practical protection against snake bites, but some depicted enemies or were used as potent magical devices. One particular snake, the Ouroboros, was depicted in a circle swallowing his tail. He was symbolic of totality, and appeared on amulets of protection or any amulet requiring totality.

Many deities were pictured with, or represented by, a serpent form. The snake illustration on the left symbolizes destiny and represents the god of destiny, Shai. Depending upon how many loops the snake has, it has a different meaning. Trying to decipher the different snake portrayals has been a challenge for Egyptologists.

The cobra, shown above on the right, was given royal status and goddesses reflected the cobra's might. There were two royal cobras, both depicted as female. One, a goddess of predynastic times named Edjo, symbolized sovereignty over Lower Egypt and was drawn as a human woman. The second goddess, named Nekhbet, ruled Upper Egypt and was drawn as a vulture or a cobra. The cobra was a popular deity form whose chief duties were protection, granting dominion, and spitting fire against enemies.

The amulet of the cobra was called a *uraeus* and was worn on the brow, attached to fillets or to the crowns of all royalty and gods. The cobra was placed on funerary masks, skullcaps of royal mummies, and added to other amulets, such as the Eye of Heru. Numerous *uraei* lined the columns and upper walls of temples and other buildings.

A wooden figurine of 1700 B.C. found in a tomb under the Ramesseum at Thebes is a lioness goddess (or a priestess in her form) holding metal serpents that were employed in magical rites. This proves that serpent forms were used in magic, but it is not known how they were used.

Serpents were also used to threaten enemies in Egyptian mythology. Auset sent a serpent to bite Ra in order to learn his secret name. Ra was challenged by a monster serpent god named Apep. Serpents were consorts of the hostile god, Set. Some magical papyri have pictures of a pantheistic deity trampling serpents and other dangerous creatures under foot.

Serpents were made out of various metals and stones. Red stone, red jasper, and carnelian were popular materials. You can make serpent amulets to wear or carry, or use them in pictures and figures for magic. Their use is varied. Like many symbolic creatures, they are considered as either good or bad and can be used in any type of magic.

Solar Eye

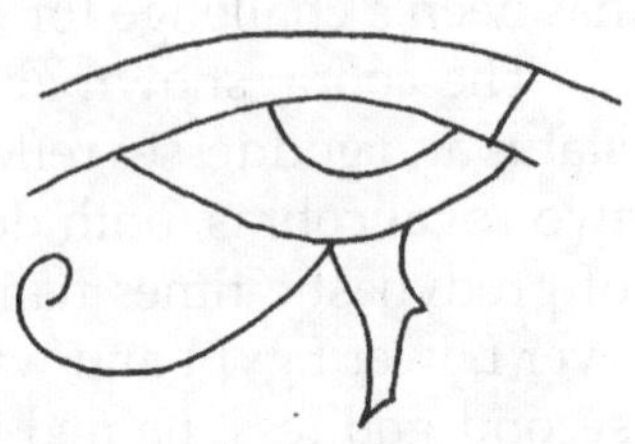

The solar eye is the powerful eye of the Sun god, Ra, and is personified as a goddess who defeated the enemies of order and light.[11] The Eye of Ra has many goddesses who embody its power. The three most important used in magic are Het-heru, Sekhmet, and Weret-Hekau. It is one of two great amulets used in magic. The other is the Eye of Heru—the Moon eye. In Egyptian mythology, the two are often considered identical in meaning and power. It is frequently difficult to identify which eye is being depicted in Egyptian pictures, because the two were often drawn alike. The solar eye is the right eye, and the moon eye is the left eye. Often, both were shown together to form an amulet issuing the healing power of Heru and the protective power of a mighty eye goddess, such as Sekhmet.

This amulet derived from the creation story of Egyptian mythology. In the beginning of existence, there was darkness. The god Ra-Atum had two children, the air god Shu and the moisture goddess Tefnut, who ventured out into the darkness to explore. Fearing he had lost them, Ra-Atum removed his divine eye from his fore-

---

[11] Geraldine Pinch, *Magic in Ancient Egypt*, p. 180.

head and hurled it into the darkness to find them. His eye became the Sun, and was known as the solar eye that lit up the darkness.

This eye was often drawn on the front of magical papyri to protect magical words and charge them with great power. It was used in love spells to cause a couple to separate so the magician could procure his desire. In a Graeco-Egyptian magical papyrus, a spell survives in which the magician invokes a goddess embodying the power of the solar eye to infuse with power a scented oil he will use as an aphrodisiac.

Traditionally, the solar eye was made out of green and black faience, granite, porcelain, silver, and many other materials. You can make the eye out of stone, wood, or papyrus to wear as an amulet. Drawing it upon magical papyrus, alone or with other amuletic pictures, is both traditional and effective. Use the solar eye in love spells, to charge magical tools or scripts, for protection, and in defensive magic.

Djed Pillar

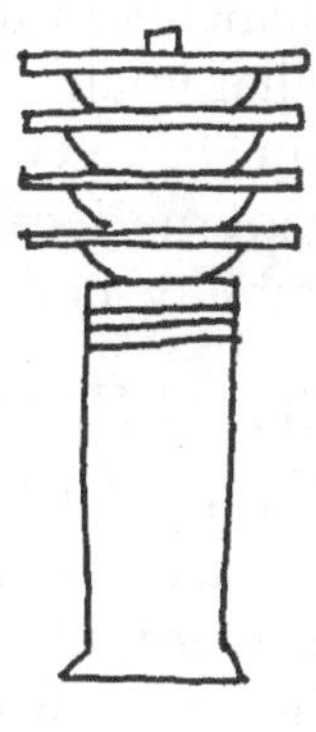

The djed pillar became the most important religious symbol in Egypt. The ceremony of constructing the djed pillar at Djedu (later known by the Greeks as Busiris) symbolized the reconstituting of Ausar's body, which was a most dignified ritual in connection with the worship of Ausar. This ceremony reflected the mythological story of Heru carrying out funeral rites for his father, Ausar, by raising the sacred pillar to assist his father's resurrection to become king of the underworld. The ritual raising of the djed pillar became traditional at certain festivals.

The pillar receives its name from the town of Djedu in Egypt where the oldest-known cult of Ausar existed. Its significance is not entirely known. It may have represented a sheaf of corn in agricultural rites, as Ausar had an aspect as a corn god. Later, the pillar was a sacred relic representing Ausar's backbone, symbolizing endurance, strength, and stability. Some Egyptologists think this amulet represents the tree trunk that Auset used to conceal her husband, Ausar's, body from Set in Egyptian mythology.

The four cross bars on the pillar mark the four cardinal points, giving it both religious and magical significance. The djed pillar was worn as a protective and strengthening amulet. It was often placed on a necklace with protective animals, the ankh, and the Eyes of Ra and Heru together. Ancient magicians likely included the djed pillar in magical scripts, especially if invoking hostile deities or beings. By stating that he possessed the pillar, the magician claimed to possess Ausar's backbone, which frightened unworldly beings into submission.

This amulet was made from various materials. The tomb of Queen Weret, dating of the l 2th Dynasty, contained elements of a bracelet she wore which included the djed pillar inlaid with carnelian, turquoise, and lapis lazuli. You can shape your amulet from any material, or draw it onto papyrus. It can be worn or used in magical scripts to acquire stability, endurance, and strength.

Eye of Heru (Moon Eye)

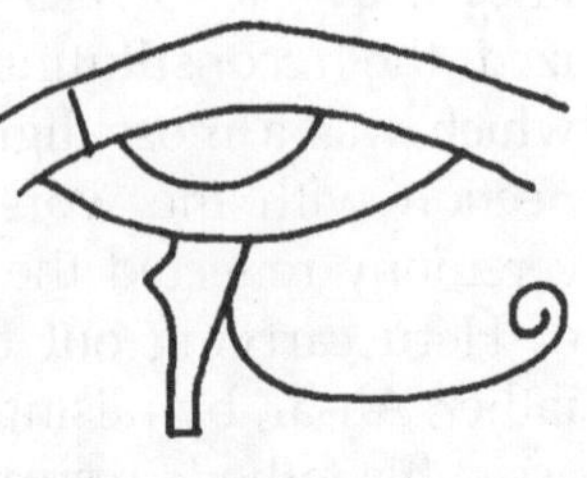

The Eye of Heru was a common amulet in ancient Egypt, and is worn as a pendant today. In Egypt, it was called the *wedjat* and is worn to bring blessings of strength, vigor, good health, and luck to its owner. Above all, it is an awesome symbol of protection. In mythology, Set injured the lunar eye of the sky god, Heru. Tehuti, with his great intelligence and magic, restored Heru's eye so that it represented totality and health. (In other papyri it is Het-heru who restores Heru's eye).

Eyes were very important to the Egyptians. They believed that the eye was the mirror of the soul. An Evil Eye was the opposite of the Eye of Heru. It mirrored deceit, bad intentions, and threatened imminent danger. The power of the Eye comes from Heru, who maintains a role in Egyptian magic as a victim and a savior. He offers his power to humanity for defense, healing, and to establish order. Heru was represented by a falcon. It is believed that his right eye was the solar eye, and his left eye was the lunar eye. Together, the eyes create a powerful, indestructible amulet. (See the illustration of the pectoral amulet, below.)

The archetypal amulet was the wedjat eye. Scribes of magical papyri often instruct that it should be drawn on papyrus or linen as a temporary amulet. Funerary ceremonies include spells for charging the Eye of Heru to protect and empower the deceased. Magical scripts have spells for using the Eye to protect the magician, and to seek out the identity of thieves.

The Eye of Heru was usually made from lapis lazuli, jasper, silver, wood, porcelain, carnelian, and, in some cases, it was plated with gold. The lunar eye, or an amulet of both eyes, may be worn to acquire amuletic power or drawn on papyrus in magic.

Pectoral Amulet

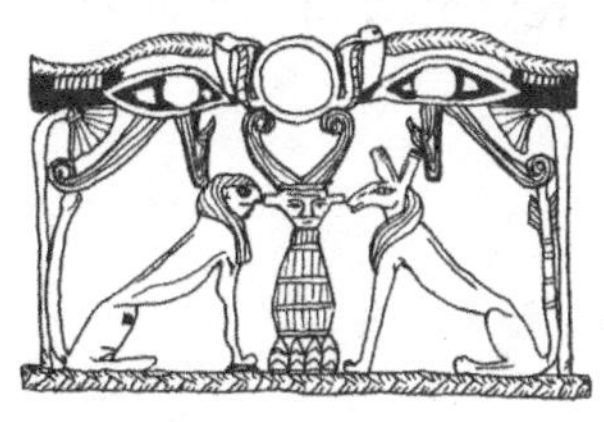

More complex and decorative amulets were made by incorporating different symbols together on one piece or jewelry, or in a magical drawing. You can combine the amulets herein to create your own powerful amulets for use in your magic. Above is an example of a pectoral from a 12th Dynasty necklace. This pectoral is said to come from

Dahshur in Egypt and is now kept at Eton College in Windsor.

In the pectoral's center is a representation of the goddess Bat, who personifies the sistrum of Het-heru. To her left is Heru, represented as a sphinx. To her right is Set, who appears in an unknown animal form. Curiously, the two gods are unified as allies to protect the royal owner of the pectoral, instead of in their mythological roles as enemies. On Bat's head is the Sun disk guarded by the Edjo and Nekhbet cobras, or uraei. On each side of the disk are the eyes; on the left is the Eye of Heru and on the right, the Eye of Ra.

Thousands of individual and combined amulets existed in ancient Egypt. There are amulets that depict limbs and organs of the human body. The fist, hand, and finger amulets probably derive from magical gestures. Amulets were used in medical spells, including decrees that named the ailing parts of the body and commanded them to become well. The Egyptians even used incised seals as amulets. These were commonly in the form of scarab beetles and were used to seal chests, boxes, and documents. In magic, scarab seals were used in written magic to symbolize divine authority and protect magicians from harmful forces. Some Egyptian amulets survive to which we cannot assign a specific magical use. These may always remain a mystery, perhaps to be revealed only by devoted, contemporary magicians.

Chapter Four

Writing and Using Magical Script

maȧ kheru
He who realizes his Word.

The divination and magical scripts of Egypt survive for our use on numerous items—tomb walls, statues, funerary objects, furniture, amulets, vessels, and long rolls of papyrus or leather which are considered books. Words of power, magical names, the art of writing, and the scribes were the backbone of Egyptian magic. Each was believed to be divine and fundamental to magic.

The importance of words of power and magical names in magic can best be understood through Egyptian mythology. The god Tehuti is the god of intellectual pursuit in both the sciences and arts. He is a master magician. He invented hieroglyphic writing which, in the Egyptian language, is called *medoo-neter*, "the words of the god." Tehuti acted as both a scribe and messenger to the gods.[1] The Egyptians believed that he created

[1] Barbara Watterson, *Gods of Ancient Egypt* (New York: Facts on File, 1985), p. 180.

their language and writing, and gave it to them for their use. These skills were acknowledged as effective, not only in mundane communication between people, but in altering a person's physical, emotional, mental, and spiritual existence.

The god Ra created himself, the world, and all of life by magically uttering the Word. By speaking the Word and the Name of all things, he brought them all into being. This was the root of all Egyptian magic. Like many Oriental nations, the Egyptians placed great importance on the knowledge and use of names that possessed magical power. In the East and in Egypt, the written word has long been revered. Wearing or carrying a copy of sacred writing had great power to protect or to produce certain results. Learning to use magical words and names was deemed a necessity for both the living and the dead.

Words have power. In Egypt, they acted as the magician's armor in magic. They act as channels through which thought-forms, motives, ideas, energy, emotions, and courses of action could manifest in reality and be directed. Your choice of words in any given situation presents an internal part of yourself to the world—your desires, motives, emotions, and the type of person you are. When you speak in a certain tone and say chosen words, it creates an immediate emotional and energy response in both yourself and the person listening.

The ancients recognized an active power in words beyond mere communication. Words can bring happiness or hurt. When you are depressed and a friend offers kind words, your spirits are lifted and a sense of wellbeing overcomes you. Phrases such as "verbal abuse" articulate the effective power of words.

Words are a map of the will, organizing and activating the desire of the will into the physical plane and planes beyond. Scripts for religious and magical rituals were not developed merely as a narration of the work, but as verbal channels through which the energy of the will could take shape and be directed at both the subjective and objective universe.

Invocation, evocation, and other forms of magic can be executed through your mind and thought-forms without you speaking at all, but the Egyptians preferred ceremony. Words, sounds, gestures, symbols, actions, and the theatrics of ceremonial magic provided magicians with stimulants that empowered the physical and psychic senses. Through these channels energy is raised, harnessed, and projected toward the magical aim.

No Egyptian magical spell or action is complete without a script that is spoken to charge it. Various papyri state that both spoken or written words were sufficient to produce remarkable success in magic. In this chapter, you will learn the anatomy of ancient Egyptian magical script, how to write your own script, and how to recite the scripts to achieve remarkable effects.

Magical Writing and Books

In his own hand, Tehuti wrote forty-two books containing the entire wisdom of the world. These books contained laws, information about deities, hymns, rituals, instructions for training priests, cosmology, astrology, medicine, and everything pertaining to the beliefs and practice of magic. The forty-two books and other magical papyri were hidden and viewed only by priesthood initiates. The whereabouts of the forty-two books of Tehuti is unknown.

Books of magic existed in the Royal library. These were not mere treatises on magical practices, but comprehensive works with detailed instructions on how to perform the ceremonies necessary to make formulas or words of power efficacious.[2] Although there were books on magical instruction, magicians had the freedom to

[2] E. A. Wallis Budge, *Egyptian Magic* (New York: Dover, 1971), p. 77.

design their own scripts and ceremonies. Therefore, you can confidently write your own Egyptian script to use in divination or magic and carry on this tradition.

Collections of spells, and individual spells, were ascribed to gods and sages. Many are purported to be secret scripts from the Houses of Life. A House of Life was a library, scriptorium, school, and university all in one.[3] Within the Houses of Life, specialized priest-magicians studied, taught, and practiced magical rituals, although their work was never revealed to the public. The scripts and ingredients used in magical spells were kept hidden. Moreover, each House of Life, temple, and the royal palace had a library.

Egyptian magicians indulged in showmanship and different Houses of Life and individual magicians did not usually exchange magical scripts whether for financial or egotistic reasons. Commoners sought out the most successful and renowned magician at a time of dire need, so reputations were very important to maintain. Magicians belonging to a particular House of Life also had private scripts and practices. It was common for a magician to practice magic for himself as well as for individuals who solicited his help.

When Egypt was finally conquered by invaders bringing the new religion of Christianity, most of the magical books were destroyed. The Emperor Augustus (r. 30 B.C.–A.D. 14), considered works of divination and magic politically dangerous and was a central figure in their destruction.

Egyptian Scribes

Not all scribes were magicians. Some wrote law books and business-related documents for the pharaoh, land-

3 Geraldine Pinch, *Magic in Ancient Egypt* (Austin, TX: University of Texas Press, 1995), p. 52.

lords, and business owners. The divination, magic, and religious scripts were written by scribes that were magician-priests.

As the god of writing, Tehuti was associated with all scribes. Through this connection, scribes had a position of great power in both common government and religious-magical work. Scribes honored Tehuti. He created their palettes and ink jars and provided them with papyrus and calf leather to write on. As a libation to Tehuti, at the start of their daily work, scribes poured a drop of water onto the ground from the palette container where they dipped their reed pens.

As a modern Egyptian magician, you are also a scribe. You are able to use the ancient spells that have survived thousands of years or you may write your own. If desired, you can use the same writing and recording utensils used by the ancients.

Writing Utensils of Scribes

Scribes used palettes, which were rectangular and usually made of wood, but sometimes of basalt, ivory, or stone. These palettes measured from ten to seventeen inches in length and two to three inches in width. Two round cavities were carved into them, usually on the right, to hold red and black ink. A groove with a sliding top held reed pens. Palettes were often decorated with inscriptions praising or invoking Tehuti that were carved, written in ink, or inlaid in color. The name of the palette's owner was usually added. Figure 10 (page 98) shows what a palette looked like.

The Egyptians wrote magical script, hymns, and praises to the deities everywhere—on statues, coffins, tomb walls, obelisks, and elsewhere. For daily writing of spells and religious rituals, papyrus and calf leather was used.

The tall papyrus reed was bountiful along the Nile. It grew along the banks and in the delta's marshes. Papyrus sheets were made by laborers who pulled flat strips

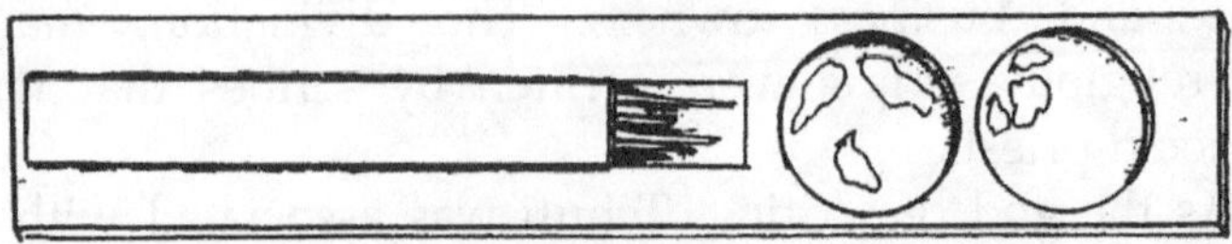

Figure 10. Scribe's wooden palette (with ink and reed pens).

of the reed's pith and laid them in two perpendicular layers. When these two layers were moistened, then pounded smooth and dried, they made a smooth surface to write on not unlike paper. Sheets of papyrus were pasted together to form scrolls, which served as books. These were stored in jars or boxes to prevent deterioration. Egyptians did not have books that resembled ours with covers and individual pages.

Calf leather was used for formal documents, especially those for temple libraries. The calf leather was not as durable nor did it hold ink as well as papyrus.

Egyptian inks were made of vegetable substances, of specially prepared copper, and colored earths. While the method for preparing such writing inks is not known, you can use herbs and plants available today to make similar natural inks.

How to Make a Palette and Writing Ink: You can make your own palette out of wood, using the description given above. Using a chisel or gouge, carve out the long groove to hold your pencils and pens. If you wish you can use natural inks and a stiff grass shoot similar to a reed pen. A quill pen or sable paintbrush is an appropriate substitute for the reed pen. Reed pens are difficult to obtain today, but may be found by contacting the companies listed in the resource list.

The pokeweed is probably your best choice for making writing ink. It is a North American weed with purplish-white flowers, reddish-purple berries, and poisonous roots. You can purchase the seeds or plants from some nurseries and herb sellers. Collect the berries from the plant and mash them to make a blood-red ink. (Contemporary ceremonial magic spells use pokeberry ink as a substitute for dove's blood.) Sources for authentic papyrus sheets can be found in the resource list. The mail order companies listed acquire the papyrus direct from Egypt.

The Anatomy of Egyptian Magical Script

This section provides you with an understanding of the anatomy of written and spoken script so that you can use the spells presented in this book and create your own effectively.

It was the hope of the magician to imitate the creator's powerful utterance of words that had prompted all gods and life into existence. Through words, the magician sought not only to summon gods and other beings, but to control them do to his bidding.

The actual words spoken in a spell are called scripts. The instruction of how to use the script is called the rubric. In script for divination and magic, every single word and sentence serves a purpose for the magician. There are four primary uses of words of power in Egyptian magic:

- To invoke gods, goddesses, or unworldly beings by the use of magical names;
- To enable the magician's mind to focus and concentrate to work magic;
- To shape-shift into a god-form or being-form to work magic;
- To charge a talisman, amulet, or spell.

Some spells begin with a dialogue between two gods, a short mythical story, or with an invocation. In an invocation, a god is called to intervene on behalf of the magician or the seeker for whom the magician works magic, or to be commanded into action as desired by the magician.

The scripts repeat assertions and commands several times, which prompts and requires concentration of the magician's will. It was thought that, by stating the desired results of the magic repetitively and with intense concentration, the results would indeed be realized. Through this process, the client of a magician became convinced, with great confidence, that the magician's spell would succeed.

Negotiations and threats are also found in many magical spells. Threats were not meant as malicious, but as an enforcement of a divine contract the magician believed was made with deities during magic. Sometimes the invoked deities were threatened with abandonment or desecration of their temples if the magician's will was not satisfied. Usually, threats of sending demons or vicious deities were made toward human or unworldly enemies. In one such spell, the aggressor is to be stuck with the arrow of the goddess Sekhmet, penetrated by the magical power of Tehuti, cursed by Auset, and blinded by Heru.[4] Magical scripts often maintained a precarious balance between upholding the principals of Maat—truth and divine order—and tipping the scales toward chaos to achieve a magical aim.

Most scripts provide instructions on what words are to be said during phases of a divination or magical ritual, as well as the number of times the script should be recited—usually four, seven, or nine times.

Magical Names

Ra had a Great Name by which he ruled over the world and all things in full power. This name was unknown to gods, kings, and humankind. It was never spoken and re-

[4] Geraldine Pinch, *Magic in Ancient Egypt*, p. 73.

mained hidden so that no magician could ever gain power over him. One day, the great magician-goddess, Auset, plotted to trick Ra into revealing the Great Name to her. In legend, she was successful. Thereafter, Ra was challenged by other gods, kings, and magicians. At times in Egyptian religious history, he lost his absolute power to more powerful gods, whose temples consequently flourished.

Creation was the handiwork of the god Ra and the god Khepera, brought about by the utterance of the Great Name. Subsequently, it was thought that only by pronouncing a name could a person come into being on Earth. Without a name, no person could be identified in the Judgment at death. Use of a person's name could bring a curse to its owner, or a healing and blessing. The name of a person or living creature is as much a part of his or her being as the soul and other bodies. As you learned in chapter 1, a person's name was actually one of nine bodies, and was an essential part of that person's existence. It was thought that a name was the label for a worldly or unworldly creature's entire existence. That name, however, was vulnerable to manipulation by magic.

This belief is logical. Think of how rumors and gossip are spread. A person is identified by name and information, positive or negative, is connected to that name. No matter whether the gossip is good or bad, true or false, the individual will somehow be affected by the mere use of his or her name associated with the information.

In Egypt, it was believed that care of one's name was necessary, for a person could be injured by the misuse of his or her name in the same degree as by a physical wound. If an enemy knew your name, he could use it in magic to harm you. If a magician blotted out the name of an enemy and his destruction was not apparent on the physical plane, it was believed that, once deceased, the person could not be identified in the Judgment. The gods, being unable to know his or her name and utter it, could not provide the individual with a future life in the underworld.

The names of gods were channels to their supreme energy. The names of demons and other unworldly beings possessed great power as well. If the name of a god or devil was known and used to summon it, it was believed they had to answer.

This belief makes sense. If you were walking down the street and someone called out your name, you would acknowledge by stopping to take notice of who summoned you. The Egyptians believed that gods and all unworldly beings would do the same and that, at that moment, the magician could harness the invoked power to control and direct them.

Magical Names of Many Forms

Some gods, such as Tehuti, and devils, such as the renowned challenger of Ra, named Apep, were believed to have the power to assume different forms. Each form had a unique name. To gain absolute power over a being that changed forms, it was vital to know all of the form-names.

The magician frequently shape-shifted during divination and magic to a god-form, a devil-form, or to the form of a mythical creature like the griffin. The secret names of the form were recited so that the magician's transformation was ensured and completed. That is why Egyptian scripts contain an abundance of magical names to recite. In certain papyri, Egyptologists and translators have had difficulty in deciphering all the names' meanings, and in determining to which god or devil-form they pertain.

How to Sound Magical Words and Names

The greatest asset in using words to amplify the power of your will is sound. It provides an intensity to your motive and energy toward a magical aim.

Egyptians recognized sound as a direct channel between humanity and the gods. They knew that the practice and use of sound in the words and names of scripts revealed the real mystery of magic. Proper pronunciation and recital of magical script was one of the most important principles in working magic. Aside from ritual tools and appropriate gestures, they believed that, if words of power were not spoken, the magic would not succeed.

How is it possible for us to learn to speak the Egyptian's language fluently and properly? Learning their ancient language could take years and the results of our study could not be guaranteed to be precise. This obstacle can be overcome for modern students by the translation of ancient texts into English and other languages. These allow you to recite the words of power in your own native tongue. Magical names that remain Egyptian can be vocalized to sound as they did thousands of years ago.

Magical words and names can be vibrated in vocalization as you would any mantra. Emphasis on each syllable, so that you can hear it resonate and feel it vibrate within you, is the key. The sound of any power-word or name seeks and harnesses that power. When this sound is combined with concentration and visualization, you stir the energy and power to which you are heir as an Egyptian magician.

Sound is a form of energy. Different vibrations of sound cause varying energy levels. Your state of consciousness can be changed by your own vibrational rate. You can also obtain visions of the gods and shape-shift, (see page 105). When sound is used as a mantra, your concentration, visualization, and power during magic can be accelerated.

The rate of vibration in your pronunciation of words and names changes energy molecules. Every cell of a thought, emotion, plant, animal, person, and all that is visible and invisible, vibrates, because every atom of every molecule within a cell is energy. All that is animate and inanimate consists of energy. The human voice produces two different sound qualities: consonants and vowels. Each quality releases and enhances the energy of your consciousness and therefore empowers your divination or magic work.

The divination and magic scripts you will use in later chapters were written by ancient scribes who often specify that certain scripts be said in a "drawling" voice. Egyptologists are uncertain precisely what "drawling" means, but it is certain that vocal tones were altered throughout scripts to produce vibrational and energy-raising effects. In my personal practice, I interpret "drawling" as a lengthening of the words spoken to produce vibration—like singing each word, and emphasizing syllables. This has tremendous power. The vibrational levels are highest and the energy of the magical work can literally be felt rising.

Because the names of gods and unworldly beings have been used repetitively for thousands of years, a direct link has been established between the human and divine levels of existence. You can tap into this link by learning to vibrate the sound of magical words and names out loud and internally. With practice, the exercise below will enable you to become adept at the pronunciation of magical script.

Pronunciation Exercise: Anpu is a popular god that is invoked in both divination and magic scripts. He has many magical, secret names. You will practice with his secret names that appear in Col. XIV of *The Leyden Papyrus*. These names appear frequently in other ancient papyri as well. Assure that you have privacy and a quiet environment to conduct this exercise. The secret names of Anpu are: Pisreithi, Sreithi, and Abrithi.

1. Prepare your mouth and throat for making the sound of the first name.

2. Relax. Inhale deeply, then release the air steadily from your body.
3. Look at the name. In your mind, or even in a whisper, practice saying it until you pronounce it in a manner that feels right.
4. When you speak the name, allow equal emphasis for each syllable.
5. Say the name slowly. Once you can sustain the sound and vibrate the name audibly for ten seconds, cause the name to vibrate silently within you. With practice, you will feel the vibrations of the sound of the name resonate within you.

Try sounding each of Anpu's three secret names with this exercise. Once adept at this exercise, try to inhale and vibrate the sound of the name within you, then exhale and make the exact same vibrated sound through actual vocalization of the name. When using Egyptian script, it is ideal to use this method when reciting magical names for invocation or shape-shifting. By sounding the names of the gods and beings that you invoke, in conjunction with shape-shifting into a god-form, you can best facilitate the powers of the cosmos and the power inherent within you for working magic.

Shape-Shifting Instructions in Scripts

Shape-shifting is included in the ancient scripts of chapters 5 and 6. It is crucial that you learn and practice this magical art.

What Is Shape-Shifting?

Shape-shifting is a very real phenomena that uses the ka/double body. Contemporary magic scripts call this body by many different names—the astral body, the magical body, and others. Every living creature has a double body and can learn to use this body. It is the double of your physical body, its subtle body of energy, which can manifest into magnificent forms of energy.

By altering the energy field of the double body, it is possible to shape-shift, because human beings operate on levels beyond the mere physical. You sometimes experience an alteration of energy and consciousness while driving your car, when suddenly you realize that you have traveled a distance, but your mind was not focused on the actual driving. It had wandered into daydreams or other conscious states, and you experience a real feeling that your driving ability was operated by some "automatic pilot" area of your mind. Although physically and consciously driving, your consciousness shifted slightly and your mind escaped the physical plane to enjoy thoughts and images on different levels.

You alter your moods, mannerisms, reactions, and mental focus daily. During a stressful day, your mind may take a break from physical reality and wander into daydreams. Your ability to alter these qualities of yourself is the basis of shape-shifting.

The ability to project out of your physical body is known as astral projection, which is similar to shape-shifting. You have a body of energy, often termed "the body of light," which, by your concentration and command, can shape-shift into any form.

Egyptian Shape-shifting Ideology

By using the ka/double body, Egyptians shape-shifted into gods, animals, unworldly creatures, and objects to work protective magic, to intimidate an evoked hostile being, for divination and spying, and certainly for other unknown purposes.

When you project your double body into the form of an animal, you truly become that animal, which can serve you well in defeating an evil presence beyond the physical plane. You could shape-shift into a night raven to fly through the celestial sky to obtain a divination vision or to spy on an enemy.

When the Egyptians built a talisman, or any figure of a god or goddess, they believed that the god's spirit and power resided in it. The power lasted as long as the object was intact and any symbols, gods' names, or emblems were not erased from it. The enormous statues of gods at temples or tombs were talismans in which resided the spirit and protective power of the deity.

Egyptians believed that it was possible to transmit the double body of a man, woman, animal, or living creature into a figure. If you make a statue of someone with whom you wish to have a relationship, you can transmit that person's qualities and characteristics into the statue for magical purposes.

Magicians practiced an improvised dialogue with gods, spirits, or unworldly beings. Usually, this was conducted after the magician introduced himself as a god-form or other being-form, which he did through shapeshifting. By shape-shifting, the magician was able to confidently negotiate, overpower, and control the approached god or being in order to carry out his will. The magician was also able to deliver ultimatums to deities while protected by the disguise of another form.

Egyptian Methods

The Egyptians practiced two methods of shape-shifting: the use of magical oils, and the shifting of consciousness. The use of oils appears in many prescriptions of the medical papyri. Physicians used oils to heal, and magicians borrowed their knowledge and use of oils for both good and harmful results in magic. Magician-priests used oils in the temples for the performance of important religious ceremonies. Magical oils allowed magicians to shift consciousness and shape-shift quickly into god-forms and mythical creatures in order to acquire optimum magical power.

The use of oil for shape-shifting is described in the text *Lucius sive Asinus*.[5] Lucian provides us with an account of a woman who used a magical oil to transform herself into a night-raven. She undressed, lit her lamp, into which she tossed two grains of incense, and recited words of power over the lamp. Next, she walked to a large chest in the room that contained many bottles of ointments and withdrew a bottle, from which she took magical oil. She proceeded to rub her body from head to toe with the oil and, in a short time, she was transformed into a bird—her nose replaced by a beak and her skin covered with feathers. Once she realized she was completely transformed, she flew up into the air, gave the shriek of a raven, and flew out an open window. In the same book (page 466), the scribe gives another spell in which the magician is transformed into an ass by the use of bewitched oil.

Magical oils were made from extracts of plants, particularly herbs, and even the organs and blood of particular animals. The toxicity and drugging effects of certain plants were easily absorbed through the skin. The oil of nutmeg was made from the aromatic kernel (nut) of the fruit of the East Indian tree, which was grated and placed in a base of vegetable or other natural oil. Nutmeg oil was used in scrying over a bowl of water or vegetable oil. It is very toxic. It should not be used in excess, added to bath water, or inhaled for long periods of time. Another oil recipe might have been a mixture of aconite, cinquefoil, and hemp, which must also be used with caution because of its toxic effects. Using such ointments excessively can cause dangerous physical symptoms, such as shortness of breath, irregular heartbeat, and delirium.

Magicians did not require hallucinogens. Assuming god-forms was possible by disciplining the mind to concentrate and shift consciousness to a trance state. Re-

---

5 E. A. Wallis Budge, *Egyptian Magic*. p. 204.

peating the recital of the secret names of the form that the magician desired, induced the required state of mind for the transformation.

Shape-Shifting Exercise

In the scripts in which you recite that you are a god-form, such as "I am Seb, heir of the gods," you are actually performing a self-invocation by assuming the characteristics of a discarnate being. Words of power and the magical names of your chosen god-form act as channels through which your double transforms into the deity or being. You should study and know the characteristics of your chosen god-form or being-form. This is essential for presenting yourself to the gods, but also for projecting your energy through that form with great power.

Like any religious ritual, divination, or magical spell, shape-shifting requires a private, quiet, and relaxed environment. Sudden interruptions, such as a ringing telephone, will immediately destroy your progress, creating frustration and failure.

As ceremonial magicians, the Egyptians used incense, lamps, and images such as statues to focus the mind and to act as channels. Physical props stimulate the physical and psychic senses. They also keep the conscious mind occupied while deeper levels of the mind awaken. A shift in consciousness can thus be obtained. You may choose to use such enhancers or nothing at all. Shape-shifting is an act of the mind that can be accomplished without ritual tools or physical images.

Dress comfortably. Do not wear tight clothing, which can cause your mind to focus on your physical body. Physical sensations of the skin should be avoided.

How to Shape-Shift Using Script:

1. To begin, you may sit or lie down. Assure that your spine is straight. Your comfort is important. Relax.

Stretch out your arms and legs, and any groups of muscles that are tense. Breathe slowly and evenly.

2. When you are relaxed and ready, close your eyes. Thought-forms will evolve in your conscious mind daily reminders or worries. Acknowledge each thought-form, then let it go. Clear your mind and silence your thoughts.
3. Practice shape-shifting by using the script below, which is taken in part from Col. II of *The Leyden Papyrus*. It demonstrates a typical phase in Egyptian script when shape-shifting takes place. The script begins with an invocation of Anpu, who is frequently invoked for assistance in divination and magic.
4. Read the following script and memorize it. It is best to recite script without glancing at a book or notes, which can disrupt your concentration. "Hail! Anpu, come to me, the High, the Mighty, the Chief over the mysteries of those in the Underworld, the Chief Physician, whose face is strong among the gods, thou manifest thyself in the Underworld before the hand of Ausar. Come to the Earth, show thyself to me here today—for I am Auset the Wise, the words of whose mouth of mine come to pass."
5. Repeat this script seven times. Egyptian script is always repeated four, seven, or nine times. Repetition allows time for the words to prompt your mind to focus and shift consciousness for the work.
6. Introduce yourself to Anpu as Auset the Wise. Through speaking the words and repeating them, you not only claim you are Auset and speak as Auset, you become Auset and greet Anpu in the Underworld.

When reciting, use the techniques of sound and vibration discussed earlier. Say Anpu, Ausar, and Auset by placing emphasis on the syllables of the names during invocation. Say each slowly, "drawling" the sound. Anpu should sound something like "OOOONNNN . . . POOOO," in English. Practice saying it aloud. Can you feel the vibrations of his name physically in your throat and mouth, and the sound resonating within you? There is power in his name. You must practice saying it in different vocal tones to feel it. When you feel his power, you are pronouncing his name correctly.

Practice saying Ausar and Auset aloud. Auset should sound similar to "AAAAHHHH . . . SSSSEEETTT," in English. Vibrate the syllables in the same manner as above. When you speak a deity or mystical creature's name, think of the meaning of its force and visualize the attributes of the subject in your mind's eye. Feel the resonating vibrations of the god or creature's power within your mind, then project the feeling outward to your being so that you sense becoming that god or creature.

The Effects of Shape-Shifting: After shape-shifting into Auset in the above exercise, you may look down at your double body and find yourself appearing as Auset, or you may simply feel as Auset. Both results are positive.

For some individual's the actual process of shape-shifting may take place. One student told me: "My arms felt strangely numb, then the rest of my physical body. It frightened me, so I opened my eyes and looked down at my physical body. It is difficult to describe in words—I had separated from my physical body and it almost appeared foreign to me." This student had abruptly ended her shape-shifting by shifting her mental focus to her fear of the unusual sensation.

There is nothing to fear in shape-shifting. Different individuals experience different sensations of the double body separating and taking on the desired form. A sensation of numbness, cold, or an odd feeling of separateness from the physical body and plane is common. With practice, the sensations become identified as signals that the shape-shifting is occurring and successful.

There are modern books that state that if your physical body is disturbed, or you are suddenly interrupted during shape-shifting, it can be harmful to your physical and mental health. There are short-term effects; if suddenly interrupted, your conscious mind becomes alert and adrenaline is released, causing your heartbeat to quicken. You may experience a brief nervousness. The same symptoms might result if someone jumped out of a closet to scare you. To avoid any such unpleasant symptoms, ensure that you will not be disturbed suddenly by noise or family members, visitors, and pets.

How to Work in Shape-Shift Form: No matter the form you choose for transformation, once the shape-shift is complete, a mystical, unworldly reality unfolds. In contemporary books of magic, this plane is called the astral plane. The deity or creature invoked in your script will likely be immediately before you. Below are helpful hints on how to communicate with it and conduct magical work in your shape-shift form.

The astral plane has many landscapes. In Egyptian magic, these landscapes vary. The divination and magical scripts in later chapters include some landscapes that the scribe has already prepared: a feast of gods, for example, that you as the magician attend. You may also create your own landscape—perhaps of the desert, with the pyramids breaking the horizon. There is no right or wrong landscape. By using visualization, you can create or alter any landscape in which you find yourself.

Realize that, on this plane, you will experience energy-forms that can change quickly. If you invoke a god or goddess and you do not recognize the form before you, it may be the deity you invoked in a different form than expected. Each Egyptian deity has many magical names and forms. If this occurs, vibrate the name of the deity. He or she should answer. If you wish the deity to appear in a form that you recognize and know best, request it.

As Auset, in the exercise above, you may find yourself standing in a great stone temple supported on pillars with lotus capitals which are surmounted by figures of gods or cobras. The god Anpu may be throned, or standing directly before you. What now?

Vibrate Anpu's name. This is not only in order to greet him, but to identify yourself as the one who summoned him. He knows you—you are Auset. He will call you by her name, and possibly by her secret names. Anpu is willing to work with you. Allow him to speak to you. There is no need to be assertive in your communication with him, or to enforce control as a magician. You are tapping into the ancient energies of gods and beings that are very real and super-magical. Experience these ancient energies and learn from them. Do not direct the encounter excessively or try to make it follow a preconceived idea. The instructions here offer only an outline. Encounters will vary for different individuals.

Anpu will likely respond to you immediately. Communication may be spoken, but it is absorbed telepathically, not heard physically with your ears. His mouth may speak, but the words come into your mind. Gestures and body language are types of communication that you will experience and use. Communication is almost always cordial.

Be courteous whenever addressing a deity, mythical creature, or being that you have invoked to assist in your magic. Consider yourself an equal, especially if addressing a god in a god-form. Invoked divine beings will tell you how to work on their plane, give you magical advice, work magic with you, and give truthful answers to divination inquiries. Take care not to narrate their responses to you. In doing so, you will receive wrong information, even if it is what you hope is true.

While concentration, imagination, and visualization techniques are used, this plane of existence and the ancient energies you will encounter are very real. The plane, energies, and forms become fragments of your own mind when you direct them like imagined characters in a story. The deities and energies of ancient Egypt have waited a long time to be reactivated. Allow the wisdom and power to be passed to you unconditionally.

Communication Techniques in Shape-Shifting: The use of negotiation and threats should be a last resort, used only if resistance toward your magical work develops. It is wise to reconsider your magical aim, or your script for achieving it, if your invoked companion(s) refuse to assist.

When evoking demons and aggressive beings you need to use a more assertive communication and dominance. The ancient magicians readily challenged chaotic beings with threats, but also with negotiation, flattery, favors, and offerings.

Ending the Session: End your work by stating your intent to do so to your invoked companion(s). It is common for invoked beings to end the encounter themselves, which should not be considered offensive. When all is said and done, they may have no reason to continue.

Once salutations have been exchanged, you will gradually become consciously alert. You will open your eyes, finding your physical environment and body intact. You may feel sleepy or groggy. This is temporary. It usually takes a few minutes to regain full alertness and the capability to go on with daily responsibilities and activities.

Once adept at shape-shifting, you will notice that time has no existence on planes beyond the physical. You may begin at six o'clock in the evening and come out of the session at six-thirty, and yet feel as if you worked much longer. A lot can happen in a short period of time on other planes. Sometimes the opposite occurs: you come out of a working and notice an hour or more has passed, and you are surprised. Any divination, magical, or psychic work that involves awakening the deeper levels of your mind and escaping the physical world, transcends the space-time continuum.

Your ability to shape-shift is limited only by your skills in concentration, visualization, and the projection of your energy/power. The process is best learned through practice and experimentation. In most of the divination and magical scripts found here, you will conduct shape-shifting that will present you with remarkable encounters and wisdom that only the master magicians of Egypt could produce.

CHAPTER FIVE

Divination

seś re en seśit
Unbolting the door of concealed things.

Divination was considered a form of magic in ancient Egypt, not a separate practice, as in contemporary magic. Ancient Egyptian divination tools and techniques are quite different from the tarot cards and astrology used today and can be used today with success.

The Leyden Papyrus can be of great value to you. It is the latest known papyrus written in "demotic" script, which is a business script used on documents from about 700 A.D. forward. It includes very early Coptic words—"coptic" being the original native Egyptian script. The manuscript dates from the third century A.D., and contains information on magic and medicine.[1] The contents of the papyrus are thought to be much older than the actual date it was written by a scribe. Its discussion of magic includes techniques for divination and it was a main source in my research for the techniques presented here. *The Leyden Papyrus* briefly discusses medicine and ancient herbalism. In the next chapter, you will learn

[1] F. L. Griffith and Herbert Thompson, eds., *The Leyden Papyrus: An Egyptian Magical Book* (New York: Dover, 1974), Preface I.

of ancient medical practices that can be of practical use today.

Most original Egyptian magical scripts can be used today. There are a few exceptions, such as a script that calls for the testicles of a bull. Fortunately, the Egyptians had several alternative instructions for each purpose. Practical and authentic scripts can therefore be given that require the gathering of simple materials and little preparation.

Here you will learn what divination is and how and why it works. Then more detailed divination techniques and scripts are offered, so that you can understand the phases of Egyptian divination necessary to achieve success. Finally, divination scripts are provided for your immediate use. All are accurate and intact. You can take pride in knowing that you practice this ancient art exactly as the ancient Egyptian priesthoods did. You will learn divination by a vessel of oil, an oil lamp, dreams, the Moon, the Great Bear constellation, and many more.

What Is Divination?

Divination is the act of gaining insight into a present situation or question and thereby offering an indication of how the outcome of the situation may be controlled or manipulated by the inquirer. Divination gives you direction on how to achieve a particular goal, or what actions you can take to prevent an undesirable outcome. No matter what your question, you are given insight by which you can prepare for and take advantage of any situation. You determine the outcome of your own future. Divination is like a compass on which the symbols are guideposts to direct you on the road of life.

In ancient Egypt, divination was not used as a tool for self-exploration, as is often encouraged in contemporary divination practice. The Egyptian magician's primary goal was to seek answers about current situations for the purpose of making changes.

Divination can be used to predict the future, find objects and people, and read fortunes from dreams, visions, omens, and other divinatory implements. Through it, you can acquire spiritual and magical development. It is both an art and a skill. Proficiency depends on your natural psychic abilities and regular practice.

How and Why Does Divination Work?

When you note the hieroglyphs and created gods of ancient Egypt, it is clear that the ancient language of magic was expressed in images, objects, and symbols. This is also true for divination. A script or a magical spell is a symbolic act conducted in an altered state of consciousness. In divination, energy is projected through the symbol, image, or object, and examined by your intuitive and psychic mind to gain awareness. Actual divination systems, tools, and props are merely objects of focus for the magician. A divination system such as the tarot acts as a lens and a channel through which you can tap into the deeper levels of your psychic mind.

When you begin a divination, your mind shifts as you use images, objects, and symbols as focal points to occupy your consciousness. A shift of consciousness can lead to deeper levels of trance, which can open your psychic awareness, paranormal senses, and clairvoyant abilities. Through the trance state, you are able to connect with other beings, energy currents, shapes, and thought-forms. As you will note in reading the divination script here, each phase of the ritual coaxes the conscious mind to concentrate, allowing deep levels of the unconscious mind to unfold. Gradually, a trance state is achieved.

To understand how altered states of consciousness are possible, you need to understand the function of the brain. Your brain produces electrical discharges that, in medical science, appear as four brain rhythms:

- Beta rhythms, fastest in cycles per second, occur during normal waking activity,
- Alpha rhythms, less fast in cycles, occur when you close your eyes and begin to relax. This rhythm works in conjunction with other rhythms once you begin a meditative state.
- Theta rhythms, slightly slower, occur when you dream or conduct meditation or trance work in divination and magic.
- Delta rhythms, the slowest rhythms, occur when you are in a dreamless, deep sleep, or in advanced trance or psychic work.

The theta rhythm is desirable when conducting divination or magic. The realm of images can be accessed, as it is when you dream during sleep. Clairvoyance can occur and, through divination, images emerge from your unconscious levels. Theta can be obtained once you can concentrate your mind so that both halves of your brain harmonize.

Your brain consists of two hemispheres; the left and the right. The left hemisphere is that of logical thought, where input is detailed, organized, and arranged in categories. Speech is formulated here. The right hemisphere interprets shapes, is holistic and creative, and notices the totality of something rather than its details. The right hemisphere is the source of the unconscious mind, whereas the left controls the conscious mind. In most individuals, the left hemisphere is dominant. Your goal is to create a balance between the two hemispheres through concentration and visualization practice, and to obtain a synchronized pattern of activity. The greatest obstacle in achieving this balance is the "voice" of the conscious mind, which constantly monitors your behavior, offers daily reminders, and repetitively sings your least favorite song in your mind. Not only are outer distractions a concern, but also the inner distractions that the conscious mind produces.

Is what you experience in an altered consciousness/trance state during divination real? Yes. It is a reality generated by the fundamental energy vortex that sustains and shapes the universe. It has a different composition than the physical world reality. Your cognition is not limited to your physical senses. You are capable of experiencing paranormal perceptions in which what you see is not seen by your physical eyes, what you hear is not heard with your physical ears. Here you will encounter symbolic interpretations and sensory forms that prompt your mind's deeper levels to gain insight. This will allow you to decide a course of action.

Your intuition works beyond the physical present. It reveals how things might be. This is much different from using your conscious, factual memory, which informs you how things used to be and presently are. Intuition is a tool of your imagination. It enables you to take note of physical details in any given situation and interpret those details in an imaginative fashion to construct how outcomes might be and what your best course of action is. Your intuition travels beyond the space-time continuum at great speed, reaching a destination far from this material world to bring back insight otherwise unobtainable.

To properly practice divination, you must balance your thinking, feeling, sensation, and intuition. When balance is achieved, you are able to stand at the center of all levels and obtain a true, unbiased observance of the world around you. The distortions of the physical world are overcome. Acquiring this transcendent function of self provides success in your aims. Perhaps the best example of acquiring this transcendent function can be found in the psychological theory of Carl G. Jung.

Jung maintained that, for complete integration, all four mind functions should contribute equally: thinking should facilitate cognition and judgment; feeling should tell us how and to what extent a thing is important or unimportant to us; sensation should convey concrete reality to us through seeing, hearing, tasting, etc.; and intuition should enable us to divine the hidden possibilities in the background, since these too belong to the complete picture of a given situation.[2] Once this is accomplished and information is obtained through divination, you must use your judgment, feeling, and thinking to properly act upon findings.

In one script below, the magician invokes, speaks personally with, and sees the god Anpu. You can achieve this same result, but it is difficult to determine if the entity of Anpu is an internally created force or an external being. The debate is truly of no consequence, however, because what is experienced in an altered state of consciousness can be internal and also objective. Furthermore, it can be real. The ancient Egyptians believed that the astral form of a god existed in the statues and talismans they constructed. Therefore, the ability to perceive and commune with Anpu or any being in a trance state of mind is real of an energy, astral form. The imagination of a trained mind is what sets an energy form into position for divination or magical work.

Psychic abilities are increased through trance-induced divination, because the trance unlocks your mind and stimulates your inner vision and dormant sources of creativity. Through altered consciousness and your divination work, you break the barriers between your conscious and unconscious levels, which causes plans, ideas, and solutions to surface. Whether you ask a simple question or desire insight into a complex situation, this is how divination provides you with the tools to make changes or control outcomes.

---

2 Carl G. Jung, *The Collected Works of* C. G. *Jung*, Vol. 6, *Psychological Types* (London: Routledge & Kegan Paul, 1971), 2nd ed., p. 519, ¶ 900.

The ancients recognized that there was an area of the mind not accessible during waking consciousness. This concept is spoken of in Egyptian hieroglyphs and papyri. They understood that, to access the depths of the dark, unconscious levels of the mind, it was essential to learn to change consciousness at will. There are many ways of learning to induce such a change. Relaxation, concentration, visualization, and scrying are all tools that can be used to achieve a change in consciousness. These techniques are discussed below.

It is not known whether the ancient Egyptians practiced meditation and relaxation techniques. Reviewing their papyri, it appears they did not. It can be said however, that any exercise and discipline leading to relaxation of the body, mind, and emotions is beneficial. It does seem that concentration, the effects of symbolism, and visualization were used by Egyptian magicians. Therefore, we will address concentration and visualization here.

Concentration and Visualization

Concentration and visualization focuses your mind upon a basic object or symbol. Through it, you physically view the object or symbol externally, and then attempt to transfer the image to be held internally in your mind's eye.

The following exercise disciplines your mind to focus your consciousness with clarity. Concentrating on the image for five to ten minutes during practice will eventually cause an altered state of consciousness to occur. With practice, you will be able to hold a self-created image in your mind's eye and achieve the altered state of consciousness necessary. When you daydream you practice exactly this—concentrating your mind through images, giving action and energy to all that you create in your mind's eye.

Patience and practice is key. When you begin, it seems frustrating and difficult to hold a fixed image in your mind for mere seconds. Do not be discouraged. Feel confident in knowing that you will succeed with regular practice. Anyone who daydreams or fantasizes can learn to perfect this skill and use it at will.

Concentration and Visualization Exercise: Any work of this kind should be conducted in a quiet, private, and safe place, where your perceptions of the outer world are minimal. You will need a simple object, landscape scene, or a symbol, paints or colored markers, and a sheet of paper.

1. Use paints or colored markers to draw and color your chosen object, scene, or symbol on the paper.
2. Place or hold the paper at eye level. Focus your complete attention on the image. Gaze over it, examining every color, contour, and detail.
3. Close your eyes. You may immediately discover an "after-image" against your eyelids which, within seconds, disappears. From this, create an inner image in your mind's eye. Your image may not be three-dimensional or vividly clear, but these details will improve with practice. Many individuals claim to hold a "flat" image, which is fine.
4. If you have difficulty, open your eyes and look at your paper, then try again.
5. Repeat this exercise a couple of times each day.

Once adept at this exercise, use an actual object, such as an apple. Practice holding the three-dimensional image in your mind's eye. In time, you will be able to create an image in your mind's eye at will, such as the god Ausar standing within a desert terrain with a background of pyramids. Taking this a step further, you can then communicate with him or move about the symbolic landscape. Concentration and visualization are powerful tools for divination and magic.

Keep a diary of your practice and results. You can chart your progress and note important findings. Divination was performed by priesthoods or individuals who were trained in the methods and interpretations. As in ancient times, to gain the benefits of divination and magic, a high degree of discipline is required. With regular practice, you will develop and refine your natural psychic abilities. By maintaining a diary of results and insights, you will give order to your thought-forms and integrate your insights. Such practical exercises will enhance the link between your conscious and unconscious mind.

Egyptian Divination Purpose and Methods

The Egyptians practiced divination for two purposes: to inquire about the present and obtain useful information to make changes to a situation, and to beg or threaten for answers and assistance from a god to make desired changes to current circumstances. Thus the magician compelled the god(s) to do his or her will.

The primary methods used in ancient Egyptian divination were trance; mediumship; fire, water, and oil scrying; dream and dream interpretation; and oracles. The following is an outline of the preparations required once a divination is planned.

1. First, prepare yourself. It is stated in papyri that the magician must be pure for three days, and specifies celibacy and "purity from every abomination."
2. Locate a secret place to divine. This is defined as a dark, clean recess. It is specified often that the recess face east or south.
3. Gather all required divination tools. Commonly, the tools were: natron-water to purify the location, a new white lamp (or a lamp without red color; a vessel or bowl can be used instead of the lamp), a clean linen wick, lamp oil or kerosene, vegetable oil to pour in vessel or bowl,

frankincense, natural ink to write magical symbols or words of power onto the linen wick, eye-paint to place into your eyes to assist in seeing invoked deities, and, at times, a crude brick to set the lamp upon.

Magicians usually practiced divination in secret, at night or at dawn. It was thought that at these times the psychic currents were strongest.

- Place the eye-paint into your eyes when you are ready to inquire of the lamp in any lamp-divination.
- Invoke a specific god, or say a spell over the lamp. If you use eye-paint, you will see the god standing behind the lamp.
- Depending upon the divination purpose and script, repeat the spells either seven or nine times.
- If an answer is not forthcoming, threaten that the god's lamp will not be lit, and will be filled with fat instead of oil.

The script is recited seven or more times so that the conscious mind can concentrate on the work at hand. A trance state is induced. For this reason, it is very important that you follow the script specifications to obtain the best results. Depending upon the script, a god may or may not be invoked. One reason for a god not to be summoned is that the god Souchos dwelled in the liquid oil of the lamp.

There are a number of gods that may be invoked. *The Leyden Papyrus* tells us that the word "compeller" within the script refers to the invoked god who compels the gods to do the magician's will.[3] One of four gods was usually invoked: Anpu, The Opener of the Ways, Tehuti, Chief Over The Mysteries, Pshoi, a Graeco-Egyptian god of Destiny, or Khons, a Moon god called upon in Moon

---

[3] F. L. Griffith and Herbert Thompson, eds., *The Leyden Papyrus*, p. 22, 1.10.

divination. Any deity to whom you feel attuned with can be invoked. While it seems true that Egyptian scribes recorded and tested excellent scripts to be used "as is" without alteration, you may achieve the best beginning results by working with gods and goddesses that appeal to you.

Egyptian magicians divined alone, but often a young boy was employed to act as a medium. We can understand how a child, whose mind is unrestrained from adult concerns and conditioning, could provide an open mind and be a channel for insight. Only a boy who was pure and virginal could act as a medium. He worked with the magicians and acted as mediator between them and the invoked gods. Why the Egyptians did not employ girls in such work is a mystery. Most ancient Egyptian script, however, was written specifically to be conducted by men.

Today, using children as mediums might be seen as inappropriate, prompting questions as to whether the child would be frightened or was willingly taking part. In modern times, children are bombarded with stress. Those of us living in America do not live in a culture that encourages such practices with children. For a true picture of Egyptian divination practice, however, we will examine the mediumship of children.

In an excerpt taken from *The Leyden Papyrus* (Col. XXV, page 153), we learn how such a divination was worked. The ceremony was conducted in a dark place. The door was opened to the east or the south, and there was no cellar beneath the area. Light was not allowed to come into the place. The niche was purified. A new lamp with a clean linen wick was brought from a temple and set on a new brick, brought fresh from the mold and untainted. The brick was set upright and the lamp placed on it. Genuine oil or Oasis oil filled the lamp. Myrrh was offered upon a willow leaf before it. The boy's back was pushed against the opening of the niche. The magician sat on two new bricks and the boy sat between his feet. The following charms were recited over the head of the boy, as the magician covered his eyes with his hand.

The boy spoke these words to the lamp: "Te, Te, Ik, Tatak, Thethe, Sati, Santaskl, Kromakat, Pataxurai, Kaleu-panket, A-a-tieui, Makat-sitakat, Hati, Hat-ro, E-o-e, Hau, E; may they say to me an answer to everything concerning which I ask here today, for I am Harpocrates in Mendes, for I am Isis the Wise; the speech of my mouth comes to pass." He said this seven times. The boy was then questioned: "What do you see?" He told the magician what he had seen and answered everything asked of him.

The Egyptian divination script given here are those that the magician conducted alone. Below, you will learn how to use eye-paint. (Instructions on how to make eye-paint are given in chapter 3). You will also learn several original scripts that can be used immediately.

An Egyptian Divination Setup

In most papyri, instructions on how to prepare and set up materials for the divination are provided by the scribe. The process of gathering materials and preparing them was called "spirit-gathering." (This does not pertain to invoking unworldly spirits.) The following is a sample taken from *The Leyden Papyrus* (Col. III). It is provided so that you may gain an understanding of how spirit-gathering and divination was accomplished.

Spirit-gathering: You will need an oil lamp, lamp oil or kerosene, matches, a vessel or bowl for scrying, (and vegetable oil), seven new bricks, seven clean loaves (bread), and seven lumps of salt. This divination is to be conducted in a dark place.

1. Take the seven new bricks and lay them side by side, facing each other.
2. Place three bricks under your containers of lamp oil and vegetable oil and, with the other four, form a square to sit

or stand upon so that no part of you touches the ground.
3. Take the seven loaves and seven lumps of salt and arrange them around the oil in a circle.
4. Sit upon the bricks and gradually pour the vegetable oil into your vessel or bowl for divination.
5. Gaze into the oil and begin divining.

As you learned in chapter 3, seven was a sacred and powerful number in Egypt. It serves many uses in spirit-gathering and script.

Eye-paint: You learned how to make eye-paint in chapter 3. This paint is placed directly onto the eyes. Its purpose was to enable the magician actually to see any god invoked. When you desire to make an inquiry of the lamp, fill your eyes with the liquid. When you pronounce an invocation over the lamp, you will see a figure of the god standing behind the lamp. He will speak with you about any questions you wish. If the god does not come for any reason, pronounce his compulsion. He will come.

Be cautious in using any eye-paint if you are prone to an allergic reaction to any plants. It is best to test the liquid by applying it to your skin and leaving it there for forty-five minutes prior to use. Eye-paint is not a necessity. Many Egyptian scripts do not include its use.

Ancient Egyptian Divination Scripts: n t mte, "From the Midst"

In reading the scripts below, you will notice the instructions for spirit-gathering do not follow the format of earlier instructions given in this book. The scripts in this section appear in their original form, as taken from papyri. Some of the words of power, magical names, and other terms used were difficult to define or transliterate precisely. Translators of Egyptian hieroglyphs and papyri do the best translations they can. At times, however, this involves making educated guesses. The meaning of some Egyptian words will always remain a mystery.

The scripts, as recorded by the scribe upon the papyrus, were not given fancy headings. Most are labeled with simple titles like "A vessel inquiry," or "Another vessel inquiry." Each script given below contains the name of its original papyrus source. Any important notes the scribe made regarding the script and the spirit-gathering are also included. Important and foreign words of power, magical names, and other terms are defined at the end of each script—-researched in the notes of papyri translators and other reputable guidebooks.

A Vessel Inquiry of the Lamp

This script is based upon one that appears in *The Leyden Papyrus* (Col. XVIII). The scribe recorded that a physician in the Oxyrhynchus Nome (the capital of the nineteenth Nome of Upper Egypt), gave it to him.

Spirit-gathering: You will need a dark, purified, private location, an oil lamp, a clean linen wick, a band of linen threads (for knot magic, see chapter 2), lamp oil or kerosene, matches, and one brick.

1. Put the wick in your oil lamp, fill your lamp with genuine clean oil, such as commercial lamp oil or kerosene, and place it on the brick.
2. Tie your linen band around your bicep.
3. Light your lamp, and concentrate on the lamp flame for a moment.
4. Relax. Then close your eyes, and recite the following script nine times:

    Sabanem, Nn, Biribat, Ho! Sabanem, Nn, Biribat, Ho! O god Sisiaho who art on the mountain of Kabaho, in whose hand is the creation of the Shoy, favor me, may he enchant the light, for I am Fair-face [another roll says, "I am the face of Nun] in the morning, Halaho ay midday, I am Glad-of-face in the evening, I am Phre, the glorious boy whom they call Garta by name; I am he that came forth on the arm of Triphis in the East; I am great, Great is my name, Great is my real name, I am Ou, Ou is my name, Aou is my real name; I am Lot Mulot, I have prevailed, I have prevailed, he whose strength is in the flame, he of that golden wreath which is on his head, They-yt, They-yt, To, To, Hatra, Hatra, the Dog-face, the Dog-face. Hail! Anpu, Pharaoh of the underworld, let the darkness depart, bring the light in unto me to my vessel-inquiry, for I am Heru, son of Ausar, born of Auset, the noble boy whom Auset loves, who inquiries for his father Ausar Onnophris. Hail! Anpu, Pharaoh of the underworld, let the darkness depart, bring the light in unto me to my vessel-inquiry, my knot here today; may I flourish, until the gods come in, and may they tell me answer truly to my question about which I am inquiring here today, truly without falsehood. Hail! Anpu, O creature, go forth at once, bring to me the gods of this city and the god who gives answer today, and let him tell me my question about which I am asking today.

5. Open your eyes and see the light. Invoke the light. saying:

> Hail, O light, come forth, come forth, O light, rise, rise, O light, increase, increase, O light, O that which is without, come in.

Do this nine times, until the light increases and Anpu comes in. When Anpu enters your sacred space and takes his stand, say: "Arise, go forth, bring in to me the gods of this city." Anpu then goes out for a moment and brings the gods in.

When you know that the gods have come in, say to Anpu: "Bring in a table for the gods and let them sit down." When they are seated, say to Anpu: "Bring a wine jar in and some cakes; let them eat, let them drink."

While he is making them eat and drink, say to Anpu: "Will they inquire for me today?" If he says, "Yes," say to him: "The god who will ask for me, let him put forth his hand to me and let him tell me his name." When the god tells you his name, ask him that which you desire to know. When you have finished asking him, send them away.

In this vessel inquiry, the line that reads, "in whose hand is the creation of the Shoy," is believed by translators to mean "the fortune produced by the god of Fate," whose name is Shoy. There is also a goddess of Fate and Destiny, called "Shai." She is usually accompanied by another goddess, "Renenet," who is commonly regarded as the lady of fortune.[4] If you prefer, you may substitute either goddess for the god. One potential problem with this substitution, however, is found in Budge's *Egyptian Book of the Dead* (page cxxv of the introduction). Budge, in referring to the papyrus of Ani, addresses Shai as a male god. It may be that this deity is recognized to have both male and female qualities.

The line which reads: "I am he that came forth on the arm of Triphis in the East" means either the goddess Triphis, or possibly, the constellation Virgo.[5]

A Vessel Inquiry of Anpu

This inquiry is taken in part from *The Leyden Papyrus* (Col. XIV).

Spirit-gathering: You will need a dark, purified, private location, a bronze bowl, an engraving tool, water, oil lamp, lamp oil or kerosene, matches, vegetable oil, three bricks, a cup of sand, a censer, frankincense or myrrh incense, and a cloth sheet or towel.

---

4 E. A. Wallis Budge, *Egyptian Magic* (New York: Dover, 1971), p. 222.

5 F. L. Griffith and Herbert Thompson, eds., *The Leyden Papyrus*, p. 120.

1. Take the bronze bowl and engrave the figure of Anpu on it.
2. Fill the bowl with water and allow it to settle, being certain that the Sun does not reach it.
3. Pour vegetable oil over the water's surface.
4. Place the bowl on three bricks, with their lower sides sprinkled with sand.
5. Set the lighted oil-lamp to your right and the censer of fire to your left. Put incense, such as frankincense, on the fire.
6. When ready, kneel or sit, and bend over the vessel for scrying. Drape a cloth over your head, allowing dim light from the lamp and fire to reflect on the oil in the bowl.

Recite the following script seven times over the vessel as you gaze into it with concentration:

> Open my eyes; open thy eyes, open thy eyes, open thy eyes, Open, Tat; Open, Nap, Nap, Nap. Open unto me, Open unto me, Open unto me, for I am Artamo, born of Hame-o, the great basilisk of the East, rising in glory together with thy father at dawn; hail, hail. Heh, open to me Hah [say this with a drawling voice], Artamo, open to me Hah; if thou dost not open to me Hah, I will make thee open to me Hah. O Ibis, O Ibis, sprinkle that I may see the great god Anpu, the power, that is about my head, the great protector of the Uzat, the power, Anpu, the good ox-herd, at every opening of the eye which I have made, reveal thyself to me; for I am Nasthom, Naszot, Nashoteb, Borilammai, Borilammai, Mastinx, Anpu, Megiste, Arian, thou who art great, Arian Pi-anuzy, Arian, he who is without. Hail, Phrix, Ix, Anaxi-brox, Ambrox, Eborx, Xon, Nbrokhria, the great child, Anpu; for I am that soldier. O ye of the Atef-crown, ye of Pephnun, Masphoneke; hail! let all that I have said come to pass here today; say, hail! thou art Tham, Thamathom, Thamathomtham, Thamathouthi, Amon, Amon, thy correct name,

> whom they call Thom, Anakthom; thou art Itth; Thouthi is thy name, Sithom, Anithom Op-sao, Shatensro black; open to me the mouths of my vessel here today; come to me to the mouths of my vessel, let my cup make the reflection of heaven; may the hounds of the hulot give me that which is just in the abyss; may they tell me that about which I inquire here today truly, may they tell me that about which I inquire here today truly—there being no falsehood in them Makhopneuma.

When Anpu comes to you, recite to him: "Thy bull Mao, ho! Anpu, this soldier, this Kam, this Kem . . . Pisreithi, Pisreithi, Sreithi, Sreithi, Abrithi is thy name, by thy correct name." Ask him that which you desire. When you have finished speaking with him, call out to him seven times. Then dismiss him to his home with these words:

> Farewell, farewell, Anpu, the good ox-herd, Anpu, Anpu, the son of a jackal and a dog, Nabrishoth, the Cherub of Amenti, king of those.

Hame-o may mean "great carpenter," but it is difficult in translating to decide whether to give English equivalents or whether to transcribe the words phonetically.[6] A basilisk is a mythical, lizard-type of monster with a fatal glance and breath.

When you say "O Ibis," you are invoking Tehuti. In the phrase "sprinkle that I may see the great god Anpu,": "sprinkle" is actually a request by the magician that Tehuti conduct a ritual sprinkling of the floor for his reception with Anpu. You do not sprinkle the floor yourself; rather, you ask that this be done for you, as your double body stands before the heavens awaiting Anpu.

Uzat indicates the full Sun. *Hurlot* is a determinative of a locality, but of what locality is unknown. *Arian* is

---

6 F. L. Griffith and Herbert Thompson, eds., *The Leyden Papyrus*, p. 99.

believed to mean, "this bringer of prosperity."[7] *Shatensro black*, is thought to refer to a black ram.

Another Vessel Inquiry

This inquiry can also be found in *The Leyden Papyrus* (Col. XXVIII).

Spirit-gathering: You will need a dark, purified, private location, a bronze lamp, lamp oil or kerosene, a clean linen wick, matches, a bronze vessel or bowl, natron water or salt water, vegetable oil, and a clean, linen robe.

1. Go to your chosen place. Take the bronze vessel and wash it with water of natron/salt. Put a measure of vegetable oil in it. Place it on the ground.
2. Light the bronze lamp and place it on the ground by the bronze vessel.
3. Cover yourself and the vessel with the clean linen robe. (It is unclear if this means that you drape the linen robe over yourself and the vessel.)
4. Recite the following script into the vessel seven times with your eyes shut:

    I am the lord of Spirits, Oridimbai, Sonadir, Episghes, Emmime, Tho-gom-phrur, Phirim-phuni is thy name; Mimi, Bibiu, Bibiu, Gthethoni, I am Ubaste, Ptho, Balkham born of Binui, Sphe, Phas, I am Baptho, Gammi-satra is thy name, Mi-meo, Ianume.

5. Open your eyes. Ask the vessel what you wish. If you wish to make the gods of the vessel speak with you, with their mouths to your mouth, cry out "Iaho, lph, Eoe, Kintathour, Nephar, Aphoe."

The gods will make answer to you concerning everything that you ask. If they do not tell you an answer, recite this other name: "Gogethix, Mantounoboe, Kokhir-

[7] F. L. Griffith and Herbert Thompson, eds., *The Leyden Papyrus*, p. 99.

rhodor, Dondroma, Lephoker, Kephaersore." If you recite these, then they will answer truthfully.

Another Vessel Inquiry

This inquiry is also found in *The Leyden Papyrus* (Col. XXVIII). It uses the same spirit-gathering (preparation) as above, except that you place vegetable oil into the vessel and tie a linen band around your arm. Then recite the following script several times:

> Speak unto me, speak unto me, Hamset, god of the gods of darkness, every demon, every shade that is in the West and the East, he that hath died, rise up to me, rise up to me, O thou living soul. O thou breathing soul, may my vessel go forth, my knot here today, for the sake of the vessel of Auset (Isis) the Great, who inquireth for her husband, who seeketh for her brother; Menash, Menash, Menanf. Menanf.

Then say: "Menash, Menanf, Phoni," a multitude of times, followed by, "Depart, O darkness; come to me O light." Now open your eyes at once. The gods will come in and tell you answers to everything.

A Vessel Inquiry to See the Bark of Phre

This inquiry can be found in The Leyden Papyrus (Col. X).

Spirit-gathering: You will need a bronze cup or a vessel of pottery; pure water; vegetable oil; a kohl-stick (see chapter 3); a strip of male-palm fiber, natural fiber, or clean linen; and eye-paint.

1. Place a small amount of pure water and a small amount of vegetable oil into the bronze cup or pottery vessel. (You can use just oil.)
2. Bind the kohl-stick around your waist with a strip of male-palm fiber, natural fiber, or clean linen. Secure it by tying a knot at your side.

3. Have your container of eye-paint ready.
4. Carry your materials to an elevated place opposite the Sun outdoors. Put the eye-paint into your eyes and recite this script several times:

> Open to me heaven, O mother of the gods! Let me see the bark of Phre descending and ascending in it; for I am Seb, heir of the gods; prayer is what I make before Phre my father on account of the things which have proceeded from me. O Heknet, great one, lady of the shrine, the Rish-tret, Open to me, mistress of the spirits, open to me, primal heaven, let me worship the Angels! For I am Seb, heir of the gods. Hail! ye seven Kings, ho! ye seven Monts, bull that engendereth, lord of strength that lighteth the earth, soul of the abyss; ho! lion as lion of the abyss, the bull of the night, hail! thou that rulest the people of the East, Noun, great one, lofty one, hail! soul of a ram, soul of the people of the West, hail! soul of souls, bull of the night, bull of bulls, son of Nut, open to me, I am the Opener of earth, that came forth from Seb, hail! I am I, I, I, E, E, E, He, He, He, Ho, Ho, Ho; I am Anepo, Niri-po-re, Maat Ib, Thibio, Aroui, Ouoou, Iaho.

You shall receive answers for whatever you ask.

"Phre" is one of the many names of the Sun god, a personification of Ra. The Egyptians also attributed a boat to the morning and evening Sun, which sailed over the sky. We see evidence that this is the meaning within the script in the second sentence, "Let me see the bark of Phre descending and ascending in it."

The "bark" of Phre is actually a boat. The following excerpt from E. A. Wallis Budge's *Egyptian Book of The Dead* (page cxi of the introduction), suggests this is so: "In the pyramid texts the soul of the deceased makes its way to where Ra is in heaven, and Ra is entreated to give it a place in the 'bark of millions of years' wherein he sails over the sky." The bark was also represented by a portable shrine shaped like a ship in religious practice.

Note the reference to the seven Kings. The identity of the seven Kings is a mystery, but there is mention of seven spirits in chapter 17 of the *Egyptian Book of the Dead*. It is possible that the seven Kings correspond to them. Seven is a number associated with Hermonthis, the city of Mont,[8] which had an ancient principal cult-center called Montu.[9] Hermonthis is known by the modern name Armant.

The references to "Lion as a lion of the abyss," and "bull of the night, hail!" may represent an obscure lion god or bull god that ruled over and was worshiped by cult-centers in various parts of Egypt. In the line, "son of Nut, open to me," the son of Nut might be either Ausar or Set, probably the former.[10] In stating, "I am Anepo," the magician is thought to be identifying himself to be the great, or elder, Anpu.

An Inquiry of the White Lamp

This inquiry is found in *The Leyden Papyrus* (Col. VI).

Spirit-gathering: You will need a clean, dark indoor location with an opening facing east, an oil lamp, lamp oil or kerosene, matches, a clean linen wick, natural ink, a reed or other pen, one brick, and frankincense.

1. Fill your lamp with the oil.
2. You must write the following on your linen wick: "Bakhukhsikhukh," along with the figures or hieroglyphs on page 147, and the words, "whose name is hidden in my heart; Bibiou (Soul of souls) is his name." (The name is a solar name, possibly representing Ausar.)

---

[8] F. L. Griffith and Herbert Thompson, eds., *The Leyden Papyrus*, p. 79.

[9] Barbara Watterson, *Gods of Ancient Egypt* (New York: Facts on File, 1984), p. 14.

[10] F. L. Griffith and Herbert Thompson, eds., *The Leyden Papyrus*, p. 80.

3. Place your lamp on the new brick. Insert the rolled-up wick with the written magic on it and light the lamp.
4. Place frankincense on your brazier. Recite the following script seven times:

> Art thou the unique great wick of the linen of Tehuti? Art thou the byssos robe of Ausar, the divine Drowned, woven by the hand of Auset, spun by the hand of Nebthet? Art thou the original band that was made for Ausar Khentamente? Art thou the great bandage with which Anpu put forth his hand to the body of Ausar is the mighty god? I have brought thee today—ho! thou wick, thou mayest make reply to every matter concerning what I ask here today. Is it that you will not do it? O wick, I have put thee in the hand of the black cow, I have lighted thee in the hand of the female cow. Blood of the Drowned one is that which I put to thee for oil; the hand of Anpu is that which is laid on thee. The spells of the great Sorcerer are those which I recite to thee. Do thou bring me the god in whose hand is the command today and let him give me answer as to everything about which I inquire here today truly without falsehood. Ho! Nut, mother of water, ho! Apet, mother of fire, come unto me, Nut, mother of water, come Apet, mother of fire, come unto me Yaho. [Scribe's note: you say it drawling with your voice, exceedingly.]

Then say: "Esex, Poe, Ef-khe-ton" (otherwise pronounced "Khet-on") seven times. Lie down without speaking to receive your answers from the god, Bibiou. If you do not receive an answer after a few minutes, rise and recite Bibiou's summons, which is his compulsion:

> I am the Ram's face, Youth is my name; I was born under the venerable persea in Abydos, I am the soul of the great chief who is in Abydos; I am the guardian of the great corpse that is in U-pek; I am he whose eyes are as the eyes of Akhom when he watcheth Ausar by night; I am Teptuf upon the desert of Abydos;

> I am he that watcheth the great corpse which is in Busiris; I am he who watcheth for Light-scarab-noble.

Lie down again to receive your answers.

The second line of the script refers to the myth that Ausar was drowned, sunk in the waters for three days and three nights after Set tricked him into getting into a chest during a banquet, shut him inside, and threw him into the Nile. (See the Bibliography to locate a source for this legend of Ausar as god of resurrection). The statement, "Art thou the original band that was made for Ausar Khentamente," describes the linen used by Anpu to wrap the mummy of Ausar. The line, "Do thou bring me the god in whose hand is the command today. . . ," refers to one of the 365 gods, each of which presided over a day of the year. You are requesting the god who falls on the day on which you work this inquiry.

Nut is the goddess of the sky and Apet is most likely a birth-goddess. "Abydos" is a sacred place in Upper Egypt where an ancient cult-center worshiped Ausar.[11]

"I am he whose eyes are as the eyes of Akhom . . . ," probably refers to the eagle-like mummified hawk figures placed on the corners of Egyptian coffins to guard over and watch the dead. "Teptuf" is the old title of Anpu, and "desert" probably refers to "necropolis."[12] "Busiris" is in Lower Egypt, where the script states Ausar's, or the solar god's, corpse lay.

Alternative Invocations

The scribe of *The Leyden Papyrus* offers two alternative invocations for your use. Both of these are to be said after the gods are initially summoned in whatever script you are using.

In the first, you repeat this nine times: "Iaho, Iphe, Eoe, Kinta-thour, Nephar, Aphoe." The god of the day

---

[11] Barbara Watterson, *Gods of Ancient Egypt*, p. 14.

[12] F. L. Griffith and Herbert Thompson eds., *The Leyden Papyrus*, p. 54.

who takes a stand then commands you to state what you ask him of. If there is a delay, or the answer is not given to you immediately, recite this other name nine times, until you receive a truthful answer: "Gogethix, Mantou, Noboe, Khokhir, Hrodor, Dondroma, Lephoker, Kepaersore." Then, say the following names seven times: "Iaho, Eiphe, On, Kindathour, Napher, Aphoe."

The second invocation is similar, but uses the following words of power: "Arsinga-label, Bolboel, Boel, Boel, Loteri, Klogasantra, Iaho, is my name, Iaho is my correct name, Balkham, the mighty one of heaven , Ablanathanalba, griffin of the shrine of the god which stands today." (A griffin is a mythical animal with the body and mane of a lion, the head and face of an eagle, two front lion-legs with talons, and the wings of an eagle.)

Moon Divination

The fact that Egyptian magicians practiced Full-Moon divination is unknown to most people. As in contemporary scrying and the use of the Moon symbol in the tarot deck, the Moon in divination represents a period of introspection. It prompts reflective thought. In using the Moon in divination, your intuition often succeeds where reason fails to analyze a situation.

The Egyptians acknowledged the influence of the Moon upon the Earth and upon life on Earth. Its physical influence is essential to marine life, the weather and climate, and factors of agriculture. The tides of the Earth's waters are conditioned by the gravitational forces of the Moon. We can agree that the Moon does affect life on Earth. Therefore, harnessing its forces for divination and magic is desirable.

Nearly every individual can think of a certain phase of the Moon that makes him or her feel differently. There is an internal acknowledgment that some form of energy has changed, intensified, or decreased. The Moon affects our physical and etheric bodies, and arouses our psyche. At the Full Moon, there is a strange, real sense that whatever decisions we make, whatever actions we take, will have great power.

How does the Moon influence you and your world? Scientifically, the phases of the Moon cause a mutation in the Earth's electrical and magnetic fields. Many magicians and healers can sense the subtle fluctuation. As the Moon reflects the light of the Sun, it also reflects reality to your mind. It does so by stimulating your imagination and intuition to achieve psychic, prophetic thought-forms.

The Moon was considered a masculine aspect of nature in Egyptian practice. In some papyri, the scribes refer to the Moon as feminine, which is evidence that they were influenced by Greek magic.

Both of the following scripts can be found in *The Leyden Papyrus* (Col. XXIII).

To Divine Opposite the Full Moon

Spirit-gathering: You will need a high place outside to stand; a bronze, brass, or other vessel; water; vegetable oil; frankincense; a censer; and eye-paint (optional). You address the Moon when it is full, on the fifteenth day of the month. You must be pure for three days prior to the ceremony; pure from sexual contact and all abominations.

1. Fill your vessel with water or vegetable oil, or both.
2. Place the frankincense on the censer.
3. Fill your eyes with eye-paint, if desired.
4. Stand on a high place, outdoors, at night, for instance on a hillside.
5. Look into the vessel of oil or water to scry. Ideally the Moon's reflection should appear on the surface.

6. Pronounce the following invocation to the Moon seven or nine times, bent over the vessel, until the god of the Moon appears to you and speaks to you:

> Ho! Sax, Amun, Sax, Abrasax; for thou art the Moon, the chief of the stars, he that did form them, listen to the things that I have said, follow the words of my mouth, reveal thyself to me, Than, Thana, Thanatha, otherwise Thei, this is my correct name.

Khons was a Moon god of Egypt who was often referred to as "the Lord of Joy." He is the son of Amun and Mut. Although his name is not mentioned here, it is probable that Sax, Amun, and Abrasax represent him.

In 1412 B.C., the priests of Amun claimed that Thebes was the origin of the whole universe, where Amun ruled as "Lord of Time who makes the years, rules the months, ordains the nights and days." Therefore, it is fitting for him to be invoked in this script.

There is a considerable difference of opinion as to the meaning and derivation of the name Abrasax, but there is no doubt that he was a form of the Sun god. He was intended to represent some aspect of the creator of the world. The name has been recognized since the second century as being invincible and was, still earlier, believed to possess magical powers of the highest degree. The name is frequently found in the ancient Gnostic system. The meaning of the names in the last line of the script is unknown.

Another Moon Divination

Prepare as instructed above. Then stand opposite the Moon at night, and say the following, nine times:

> I am Hah, Qo, Amro, Ma-amt, Mete is my name; for I am bai, So, Akanakoup, Melkh, Akh, Akh, Hy, Melkh is my true name, Melkh is my true name . . . eternity, I

am Khelbai, Sete, Khen-em-nefer is my name, Sro, Oshenbet, is my correct name.

You will see the figure of the god in the vessel and he will then speak with you about everything that you wish.

Dream Divination

The Egyptians believed that the divine powers frequently made their will known through dreams. Thus they attached considerable importance to them. The figures of the gods and the scenes that they saw when dreaming seemed to prove the existence of another world that was not very different from the one already known to them.[13] The knowledge and skill to procure and interpret dreams was greatly valued in Egypt. It was accepted that the future revealed itself through dreams. A priest or official who possessed such a gift was given high status and received honorable recognition. From the Christian bible (Genesis: xl., xli.) we learn that Joseph, who was not Egyptian, rose to honored status in Egypt for his ability to interpret dreams.

Dreams are a pathway to your unconscious—a primary link between your conscious and unconscious mind. With increasing scientific interest in how and why we dream, researchers have produced some awesome findings. Using an electro-encephalograph machine on sleeping volunteers, researchers have learned that brainwave activity changes and that throughout the test, sleepers experienced cycles of ascending into a light sleep, then descending to a deep sleep. Four or five times a night, with normal sleeping patterns of at least seven hours, the subjects experienced an ascending level of a dream state termed "rapid eye movement."

[13] E. A. Wallis Budge, *Egyptian Magic,* pp. 213, 214.

Modern society does not credit the contents of dreams, but at least we are aware that dreams are necessary for mental and emotional well-being. Most people agree that dreams are one way all of us deal with stress in life through symbolism.

Dreams can expand your awareness by bringing the contents of your dreams to waking consciousness. If you recall part of a dream, sometimes scrying can help you to remember the whole dream. The ancients believed that scrying could produce shifts in consciousness similar to those that occur during dreaming.

Dream Interpretation

The subject of dreams and dream interpretation is extensive. We will concentrate on interpreting dreams for the purpose of divination.

When conjuring a dream for a specific purpose, as instructed here, your best tool is a journal. The moment you awake and recall a dream, write the details into a notebook. Many important details can be lost otherwise, since throughout the day, your mind will focus on other matters. Symbols and images brought to mind through dreams are described in the general divination discussion at the beginning of this chapter. Consulting a dream dictionary, or dream expert, is useless. You are your own best interpreter. Your analysis requires two levels of interpretation: an inquiry into the theme of your dream, and an understanding of the symbols of your dream. When considering the theme of a dream, look for the dream's main content or expressed point. For example, if you dream that you are being hunted, perhaps the theme is that you feel somehow under attack in an area of your life. Define the theme, then analyze the symbols and images in the dream itself.

Everyone dreams of people, places, objects, creatures—some that are known to life and others that seem an incredible form from another world. All are symbols.

To interpret any symbol, you need to consider how you feel about the symbol itself, as separate from the theme. How you objectively and logically consider a symbol does have significant impact on why it is part of your dream. No two individuals have the same feeling about, or understanding of, a symbol. That is why only you can decipher your dreams.

What does a symbol represent in a dream? Is the meaning of the dream subjective or objective? If the meaning of your dream is not obvious, it is best to consider it subjective. Step outside of yourself; ask your psyche to reveal the meaning of each symbol to you. Once you analyze each symbol independently, you can take your readings and incorporate them into your theme to interpret a complete meaning.

Egyptian Methods

Egyptian magicians desired dreams and visions in which the outcome of situations and the future would be revealed. There is script to procure dreams for self and for seekers by several methods, such as reciting magical words or drawing magical pictures. Below is a script for obtaining a dream using a lamp, taken from a British Museum Papyrus (No. 122, lines 64 ff. and 359 ff.).[14] Conduct this script at your bedtime, being certain that you are pure from food and all defilement.

Spirit-gathering: You will need a clean, small linen bag, an oil lamp, lamp oil or kerosene, matches, natural ink, and a reed pen or other writing instrument.

1. Write the following names on the linen bag: Armiuth, Lailamchouch, Arsenophrephren, Phtha, Archentechtha.
2. Fold it up and make it into a lamp wick.
3. Pour oil carefully over the linen wick, and light it in the lamp.

---

[14] E. A. Wallis Budge, *Egyptian Magic*, p. 216.

4. Approach the lamp and repeat the following script seven times:

> Sachmu . . . epaema Ligotereench: the Aeon, the Thunderer, Thou that hast swallowed the snake and dost exhaust the Moon, and dost raise up the orb of the Sun in his season, Chthetho is thy name; I require, O lords of the gods, Seth, Chreps, give me the information that I desire.

5. Extinguish the lamp and lie down to sleep.

The first three words of the script are words of power, the meaning of which is not known. The god of thunder is Set, but the name "Chthetho" is not found in relation to him in my research.

This second script to procure a dream, taken from *The Leyden Papyrus* (Col. V), is more complex. You must be pure. Choose a dark location with its face open to the south. Purify it with water.

Spirit-gathering: You will need a new, white lamp, a clean wick, lamp oil or kerosene, matches, myrrh ink (or any natural ink), a reed pen or writing utensil, one brick, a cup of sand, frankincense, and a censer.

1. Take the white lamp and place the wick in it. Fill the lamp with lamp oil or kerosene.
2. Write the following name and the figures on the wick with myrrh ink (or any natural ink): "Bakhukhsikhukh" and the figures, ⲃⲁⲭⲩⲭⲥⲓⲭⲩⲭ.
3. Lay the lamp on a new brick in front of you, its underside spread with sand.
4. Display frankincense in a censer before the lamp. Light the lamp and the incense.
5. Speak this script seven times:

> Ho! I am Murai, Muribi. Babel, Booth, Bamui, the great Agathodaemon, Muratho, the . . . form of soul that resteth above in the heaven of heavens, Tatot, Tatot, Bouel, Bouel, Mouihtahi, Mouihtahi, Lahi, Lahi,

Bolboel, I, I, Aa, Tat, Tat, Bouel, Bouel, Yohel, Yohel, the first servant of the great god, he who giveth light exceedingly, the companion of the flame, he in whose mouth is the fire that is not quenched, the great god who is seated in the fire, he who is in the midst of the fire which is in the lake of heaven, in whose hand is the greatness and the power of god; reveal thyself to me here today in the fashion of thy revelation to Moses which thou didst make upon the mountain, before whom thou thyself didst create darkness and light. I pray thee that thou reveal thyself to me here tonight and speak with me and give me answer in truth without falsehood; for I will glorify thee in Abydos, I will glorify thee in heaven before Phre, I will glorify thee before the Moon, I will glorify thee before him who is upon the throne, who is not destroyed, he of the great glory, Peteri, Peteri, Pater, Enphe, Enphe, O god who is above heaven, in whose hand is the beautiful staff, who created deity, deity not having created him. Come down to me into the midst of this flame that is here before thee, thou of Boel, Boel, and let me see the business that I ask about tonight truly without falsehood. Let it be seen, let it be heard, O great god Sisihoout, otherwise said Armiouth, come in before me and give me answer to that which I shall ask about, truly with falsehood. O great god that is on the mountain of Atuki (of Gabaon), Khabaho, Takrtat, come in to me, let my eyes be opened tonight for any given thing that I shall ask about, truly without falsehood . . . the voice of the Leasphot, Neblot . . . lilas.

6. You will see the god about the lamp. Lie down on a rush mat without speaking to anyone. Then, he will answer to you by dream.

Moses was a hero in the legends of the Jews both before and after Christ. The Christian bible (Acts: vii., 22) tells us that Moses "was learned in all the wisdom of the Egyptians," and that he was "mighty in words and in deeds." The Egyptians had great respect for Moses and his magic, which they witnessed when he parted the sea, which is written of in Egyptian papyri as well as in the bible. "Abydos" was a cult-center that worshiped Ausar. "Phre" refers to the god Ra.

Dreams can reveal insights into plans, emotions, and other peoples' motives as well as your own. Information concerning events and situations in your life can be gained from them. All of this is possible through interpreting your unconscious mind's symbolic language.

Horoscope and Numerology in Egypt

The Egyptians were superbly skilled in casting nativities. By knowing the precise moment of birth of a person, they could construct a horoscope.

The Table of Democritus

One Greek horoscope in the British Museum has an ancient note attached to it stating that the Egyptians were laboriously devoted to the art, had discovered it, and had handed it down to posterity.[15] Indeed, we have evidence that the origin of the horoscope may have been Egyptian.

In connection to the horoscopes of ancient Egypt, there was a "table" known as the Table of Democritus, from which predictions of life and death could be made. Its contents are included here as it is simple and thought very accurate (see table, page 150). *The Leyden Papyrus* (Col. xi., 1.1 ff.) gives these instruction for using the table:

> Ascertain in what month the sick man took to his bed and the name he received at his birth. Calculate the course of the Moon and see how many periods of thirty days have elapsed; then note in the table the number of days left over. If the number comes in the upper

[15] E. A. Wallis Budge, *Egyptian Magic*, p. 229.

Table of Democritus

1	10	19
2	11	20
3	13	23
4	14	25
7	16	26
9	17	27

5	15	22
6	18	28
8	21	29
12	24	30

part of the table, he will live, but if in the lower part, he will die.

It is not known if the table was used for making other predictions. If you have an interest in numerology, you may find more uses for it.

A Scout-Spreader Spell

To further support the theory that the horoscope originated in Egypt, below is a "scout-spreader spell" which can be found in *The Leyden Papyrus* (Col. IV). The meaning of its name is unknown. Note the astrological properties. This spell is worded somewhat differently than earlier scripts, clearly demonstrating Greek influences. The scribe tells us this is "A scout-spreader, which the great god Imuthes makes." Imuthes is invoked in other papyri as "Imhotp-wer (the Great), son of Ptah and Khretankh." We can assume his presence to be the same here.

This spell requires basic knowledge of astrology. With a quick study, you would be able to use this script effectively.

Spirit-gathering: You will need a wooden table (olive-wood if possible), a tunic, four bricks, a clay censer, matches, incense charcoal, myrrh-resin incense, a personal astrology/horoscope journal with the constellation alignments at the time of this divination, a papyrus or paper sheet, natural ink, a reed pen or other writing utensil.

Spend the night of the spell without speaking to anyone. Be certain you are pure from all abomination. Conduct this spell in a clean, purified room. The wooden table should have four legs and never have been sat upon by a man. The table should be clean.

1. Place the table beside you, and drape it with a tunic from its top to its feet.
2. Put the four bricks under the table, one on top of the other.
3. Place your clay censer before the table with charcoal of olive-wood (use modern charcoal) in it. Light the charcoal. Place myrrh resin on it. If you have extra myrrh, place it by your side.
4. Kneel toward the table, with your head being close to it. Speak the following script three times:

   > I invoke thee who art seated in the invisible darkness and who art in the midst of the great gods sinking and receiving the Sun's rays and sending forth the luminous goddess Neboutosoualeth, the great god Barzan Boubarzan Narzazouzan Barzabouzath, the Sun; send up to me this night thy archangel Zebourthaunen; answer with truth, truthfully, without falsehood, without ambiguity concerning this matter, for I conjure thee by him who is seated in the flaming vesture on the silver head of the Agathodaemon, the almighty four-faced daemon, the highest darkling and soul-bringing Phox; do not disregard me, but send up speedily in this night an injunction of the god.

5. The god then comes. You will see the god in the likeness of a priest wearing fine linen and wearing a nose

at his feet.[16] He then speaks to you, with his mouth opposite your mouth, in truth.

6. When the god has finished and goes away again, stand up and place a tablet of "reading the hours" (astrology journal that records the constellations) upon the bricks. You write the stars upon it (the horoscope/star alignment at the time of this divination).
7. On another piece of papyrus, write your purpose for the divination. Place this paper on top of the tablet.
8. Relax. Concentrate. The god then reveals to you the future horoscope of star alignments when your desires will be met.

"Phox" is thought to be a magical name, but its origin and meaning is unknown.

Divination to Identify a Criminal

Detective work, coupled with magic, was used by Egyptians to seek out criminals or wrong-doers. Just as modern police departments sometimes consult psychics for clues in finding a missing person or criminal, Egyptians put their psychic abilities to use for this purpose.

The criminal could be a person who broke the laws of society, or a person who had somehow wronged the magician. For example, if someone worked magic against the magician or slandered his or her reputation, or caused something the magician valued to be ruined, these spells acted as weapons to detect the perpetrator. In some cases, such spells served as a means of acquiring cosmic justice. This is a form of divination, although today we might consider it psychic magic with a specific aim.

---

[16] Apparently, as seen in late sculptures of the gods, the gods had jackals' heads/noses on their feet indicating wariness and swiftness. F. L. Griffith and Herbert Thompson, eds., *The Leyden Papyrus*, Col. IV, p. 41.

Bringing in a Criminal by Lamp or Bowl

The Leyden Papyrus (Verso Col. XV) offers this script for use with your lamp of oil, or a bowl of water and oil. In this example, we will use a bowl.

Spirit-gathering: You will need an oil lamp, lamp oil or kerosene, a clean wick, matches, a bowl, water or vegetable oil, natural ink, and a reed pen or other writing utensil. There are no specific preparation instructions given by the scribe in *The Leyden Papyrus*. It is not known for certain if the script below and its use of a bowl originated from the ruler-king Nectanebus, but it is probable. You must be pure and free from abomination before performing this rite.

1. Retire to a private, purified chamber and fill your bowl with water or vegetable oil for scrying.
2. On the outside of the bowl, write the following names of the gods, whom you invoke to bring in a criminal or an enemy: "Maskelli, Maskello, Phnou kentabao, Hreksyktho, Perykthon, Perypeganex, Areobasagra, otherwise Obasagra."
3. Once you have written the names, light your oil lamp for scrying.
4. Recite the above names over the bowl seven times. (The scribe notes: "This script will do mighty work in identifying a criminal.")

To be successful in any form of divination, you must master your mind through discipline. Try to identify areas of weakness, such as having trouble focusing your mind, and practice the concentration exercises described earlier. Daily physical exercise (the ancient Egyptian magicians walked frequently and got plenty of exercise) is difficult to begin, but highly recommended. Daily practice of concentration and visualization, and keeping a record of your progress, is also suggested. Practice, patience, and persistence are the key elements to becoming adept in divination.

Chapter Six

Ancient Egyptian Magic

my 're qme
Let a creation be made.

Ancient Egyptian papyri lead us to believe that magic was the first and foremost ritual practice in Egypt and that actual religious worship was secondary. This is very different from our spiritual and magical traditions today.

The word *heka* is usually translated by Egyptologists to mean "magic." Heka was also the name of the god of magic. He was one of the central forces that fused together the universe and ignited the first matter into life. He appears as a human man, wearing a false beard and grasping two criss-crossed snakes to his chest, in the Ausar position. He is often depicted in papyri as standing behind the throne of Ausar, or with the goddess Maat and the god Ausar. Sometimes the priest or priestess who regularly worked with this trinity is pictured greeting them. The god Heka did not have temples built in his honor. However, he did have shrines and an operating priesthood dedicated to him.

Weret Hekau is a goddess and Heka's female equivalent. Her name means "Great of Magic," and she was usually depicted as a cobra. It seems that she was represented by the snake-shaped short rods used by magicians. The actual word *heka* was used to describe the magical power that a deity, human, beast, or unworldly being possessed. Tehuti and Isis were considered the greatest magicians, with awesome heka. You would use the word heka to describe the magical power you have and use.

The word *hekau* describes a possessor of magic. Priests of Heka also worked as doctors, but "Hekau of the House of Life" were usually specialists in ritual magic.[1] You would use this word when referring to yourself as an Egyptian magician.

Akhu is another Egyptian word used for magical power. It also translates as "sorcery," "enchantments," and "spells." Akhu and heka can be used to imply creation or destruction.

In contemporary spiritual and magical practice, the gods and goddesses are generally invoked, revered, and requested to lend their power toward a magical aim. The Egyptian tradition is similar, but the Egyptians believed they could gain actual command over their gods, goddesses, any conjured entities, as well as the forces of nature by merely reciting their names, or words of power. Magicians could acquire the power of the divine by simply commanding it. Indeed, the main principle of Egyptian magic is the ability to utter words of power, coupled with the power of the will to command. Magical preparations (spirit-gathering) and scripts were all rather simple. The importance was placed, not on design of the ritual, but on the actual gestures and vocalizations.

The process by which an individual became a magician-priest was discussed in chapter 1. There are no

---

1 Geraldine Pinch, *Magic in Ancient Egypt* (Austin, TX: University of Texas Press, 1995). p. 53.

surviving training manuals for the priesthood. No levels of initiation or degrees seem to have existed. The training of priests and priestesses in magic is not believed to have included meditation or the extensive use of exercises to learn to raise and direct personal energy, as found in contemporary magical practice.

The Egyptians believed that certain individuals had a natural gift for magical work. Those practicing magic learned from others and through experimentation. The theory of the nine bodies made it possible for any man, woman, or child to work magic, because everyone already possessed access to what contemporary magical practice sometimes terms "the Higher Self." Thus anyone could raise this energy naturally.

Preliminary education required the learning of spell design, script, gestures, and ritual tools. Thereafter, all a priest or priestess had to do was to conduct the magical work of their choice. With faith in both their spiritual and magical beliefs, there was no question that they could harness the divine powers, raise and direct personal power, and make their magic succeed with little effort. It seems that Egyptian magician-priests created scripts, tested them by practice, and gained respect proportional to the success of their magic.

To be a magician required extensive study and knowledge of Egyptian religious mythology and philosophy, divination, various magical scripts and techniques, and a broad education. High status as a magician did, however, sometimes result from being a member of an affluent family. Achievements in magic and divination sometimes resulted in a temple or the pharaoh appointing an individual to official status. There may well have been teachers and apprentices as well. Judging from the solitary practice of divination and magic by magicians, it is appropriate to state that anyone with such knowledge qualifies as an Egyptian magician, including yourself.

The study of the Egyptian ritual tools, figures, pictures, amulets, symbols, words of power, and techniques of divination are very important factors to your working knowledge. Below, you will learn what magic is and how it works. Then you can partake of the Egyptian magical scripts offered.

Contemporary Theory vs. Egyptian Theory

In contemporary magic theory, there are two categories of magic: white magic and black magic. Ancient Egyptian magic does not discriminate between the two. The magician could choose to cure or harm at will. The Egyptians had potions and magical script to wound or cause the death of an enemy, as well as spells to win the favor of a woman and, at the same time, have her husband mysteriously, magically eliminated. The Egyptians also worked magic to improve agriculture, heal someone of illness and other ailments, or to win success, praise, and the love of a desired man or woman. Ultimately, it is your conscience that must decide how you use magic.

What Is Magic?

Magic is the art and science of causing change by force of will. It includes your ability to make something happen that you desire by exercising your own directed power. Magic enables you to make changes in all areas of your life.

Magic uses the powers of the human mind that are beyond what most, but not all, scientists acknowledge. There exist many systems of magic which employ symbols, objects, images, script, gestures, ritual design, and other useful props to assist the magician's conscious mind to focus and allow its deeper levels to amplify the will and energy to cause change.

Carl Jung's theory of synchronicity can help you understand what magic is and how it works. Synchronicity describes a reality wherein you, the individual, exist as a separate entity, but also as an integral part of the whole universal consciousness, in which absolute separation is impossible. This is the realm of the collective unconscious, a shared human psychic reality that we all have in common. You are a part of everything, and everything is a part of you. This is the plane upon which magic is worked and why it is successful. You may have desires that are totally different than those of the complete whole, but it is possible for you to tap into the energy of the whole and seek its influence to achieve personal ends.

How Does Magic Work?

The first step is to learn visualization techniques. The ability to produce images in your mind and to use symbols is what triggers the neurological repatterning needed to work magic. Learning to play a guitar, ride a bicycle, or use a computer are many ways in which your mind develops new paths for brain neurons to follow. The end result is that you become skilled at a task. Having learned how to ride a bicycle or work magic, you have developed and integrated your right-hemisphere, your intuitive mind, and you can succeed at the task.

Through the language of symbols, both sides of your brain communicate. Both your intellect and emotions are stimulated to assist in the process of causing change. Noting the hieroglyphs, symbols, figures, pictures, and other "props" of ancient Egyptian magic, we can understand that these were objects of focus for the magician-priest or priestess's conscious mind which provided channels by which their energy could be projected to cause desired change. It is your mind that works divination and magic. A prop acts as a lens for your mind's eye, and as a channel for energy or power. Your use of images and symbols implants concepts in your unconscious mind by which you are influenced to cause the concepts to become reality.

Your power of mind and internal energy of will are amplified through the channels. Your power then moves to more significant energy currents in the universal consciousness—the whole of reality. When your power is directed through images and symbols, it causes a change in the energy currents of the unseen, subjective whole and gradually the change materializes in our physical world.

In chapter 5, we discussed your mind's development and the ability to conduct divination. Reread the section regarding theta rhythms and the activity of the brain. These rhythms are essential to working magic. Much of that information pertains here, especially concerning the importance for the left and right hemispheres of your brain to become balanced.

Your attention in magic must be focused upon your aim or goal and on projecting the hidden power of your deeper levels of mind to create change. This is only achieved by learning to concentrate, and through practice. In magic, you will have an aim. You will conduct your spell and visualize the desired, final result. It is essential that you visualize your goal as already manifested in reality. Do not dwell on the result of your magic. You are powerful and capable. You must visualize and know that your aim is achieved.

Understand that your desires, emotions, motivations, and patterns of action will influence your magic. For example, you can work any form of magic to acquire employment, but if you sit on the couch all day and make no physical effort to make the result materialize on the physical plane, you may not be successful. The most adept magician is not successful 100 percent of the time. There are numerous reasons for this. A few are mentioned above.

The way you visualize your magical result may not be exactly the same as its actual outcome. The results of magic come into being in unexpected ways that can, at times, render a better outcome than thought possible.

To best develop your mind for magic, practice the visualization and concentration exercises offered in chapter 5. Practice entering altered states of consciousness and become able to induce them at will. This is achieved by direct experience, practice, and gaining confidence in yourself. Read books regarding creative visualization and hypnotherapy. These may offer ideas for practice and challenge your skills.

Magical Exercise

This is an advanced concentration and visualization exercise which will develop your mind. It is also an exercise in which you learn to project your power or energy as required in magic. You will need a private, peaceful place to conduct this exercise, and comfortable clothing. You may also perform the exercise without clothing if you are comfortable doing so.

A quiet environment is necessary. You need to concentrate without interruption or distraction. At times, inner and/or outer distraction is difficult to avoid. Any inner distraction that you may suffer will lessen in time as your mind learns to focus its attention completely on what you are doing. Outer distractions, such as a ringing telephone or background noise, should be eliminated.

Take your time conducting this exercise and, if possible, repeat it a couple of times at each sitting.

1. Be seated with your spine straight. Sit in a comfortable chair or on the floor.
2. Visualize a wide river with rich, dark-brown soil banks on both sides. This is the Nile of Egypt.

3. You stand a short distance away from the Nile itself and, looking upon the ground, find a crude brick. You bend over, pick up the brick, and stand, feeling its rough, gritty form and weight in your hand.
4. Inhale deeply and, as you exhale, visualize that you are throwing the brick with all your might into the Nile. Watch it splash, creating waves and ripples across the water's surface.
5. After a moment of rest, visualize that you are twice the distance from the Nile.
6. Reach down to the ground and pick up another brick. Its weight is twice that of the first brick. Feel its texture and weight.
7. Inhale deeply and, as you exhale, throw the brick very hard. Watch it become airborne and see it fall with a splash in the distant Nile water.

Practice this exercise until you actually feel the release of your power that accompanies the throw of the brick. Mastering your mind is not something that can be achieved overnight. Do not become frustrated. Take the time to practice and be patient with yourself. This is the key to success.

There are some individuals who seem to possess a gift for learning to visualize, concentrate, and execute a magical script flawlessly with good results. That is not the case for most people, however. Everyone is capable of working magic, but some individuals must practice more aggressively to obtain an altered state of consciousness where concentration, visualization, and total focus on the specific aim is possible.

Egyptian Magical Script

The Egyptians worked magic for every situation that arose in their lives. As you will learn, many of those situations are similar to those with which we are concerned in our modern era. Below are eight instances in which their magic was put to practical use.

1. Spells to protect against animals, reptiles, scorpions, evil magic, evil spirits, enemies, and for the deceased passing the perils of the underworld.
2. Spells to acquire praise from a disgruntled superior, tradesman, family member, friend, or a member of the opposite sex.
3. Spells to avert the anger of a superior or authority figure.
4. Spells for success in any area of life needing improvement, particularly business or income related problems.
5. Spells for defense against evil spirits, magic, unworldly hostile creatures, sickness, and enemies. There exist various script for producing sleep, madness, catalepsy, and death in an enemy. The ancient Egyptians did not tolerate betrayal or interference in life from an enemy.
6. Spells to acquire the love of someone who rejected you or did not readily grant a relationship. Some spells were written to break up a man and a woman so the magician could procure the woman. Most of these spells were written by the scribe for male magicians who sought women.
7. Sex magic consisting of script and recipes for ointments to assure that the partner of the magician would reach orgasm and fall madly in love with him or her. The Egyptian version is completely different from modern day sex magic instruction.
8. Spells for healing.

Written magic scripts were used for more than recital during spellcasting. Magicians hoped to absorb the heka of the spells into their bodies, which could best be done by soaking a script written on papyrus in beer to dissolve it, and then swallowing it with water.[2] This was standard magical practice in Egypt, although not very desirable or practical for modern magicians today.

In many spells, there are places where the identity of the magician and his or her person of intent is mentioned, as in love spells where the magician works to separate a woman from her husband: e.g. "until he cast out _______ (woman's name) daughter of ______ (her parents' name) out of his abode." It was traditional in Egyptian magic for the name of the magician, or anyone targeted by the spell, to be recited in this manner. This may have served to assure that the magic would be directed to the targeted individual and not to someone with a similar name.

Wax and magical figures, pictures, symbols, oils, magic ointments, spirit summoning, shape-shifting, the invocation of Tehuti to bring good fortune, and many other techniques were used in magical spells. You have learned many techniques in the preceding chapters that will benefit the magical spells you learn here.

The Egyptian Altar

Egyptians often employed wooden tables for altars. In some instances, stone altars were used. In *The Egyptian Book of the Dead*, we learn that the altar was used to hold ritual tools, offerings to the gods, and food and drink for funeral ceremonies. The altar was lavishly covered with offerings of fruit, flowers, incense, meat, breadcakes, ducks, and vessels for wine, beer, and oil. Single wax flowers and wreaths were also laid upon the table altars.

As discussed in chapter 5, the solitary magician used a wooden table to conduct divination on occa-

---

2 Geraldine Pinch, *Magic in Ancient Egypt*, p. 70.

sion. We can assume that, in most magical work, an altar of some type was used, probably decorated in much the same manner as for the funeral ceremonies, if invocation of a deity took place. Offerings were given to the gods for the purpose of acquiring favors from them. Magicians and scribes sometimes wrote their scripts at the altar, seated upon wooden chairs. There were royal and temple libraries that housed collections of religious and magical literature. These are described as being similar to our modern libraries.

You may wish to set aside a small table as a permanent altar. You may have an entire room, or an empty space in a room, to furnish with an altar and your private magical library. In the Egyptian Resources section, you will find mail-order companies that sell reproductions of Egyptian vessels, statues, and other functioning items that you can use on your altar.

The altar serves as a focal point and a symbol of the universe where spiritual and divine energies touch your life. By using the altar as a channel, your magical power is amplified into the cosmos, rippling across the celestial energies to produce change. It is also a practical furnishing, like a lectern, for such purposes as writing magical script.

As you read about Nectanebus, the magician mentioned in chapter 2, you discovered that magicians sometimes prepared and conducted magic in private. In keeping with tradition, you can maintain your own personal magical script, altar, and storage of all ritual tools.

The authentic script instructions below do not always specify whether or not an altar is used, or how it is to be decorated. You can use the example of the funeral altar to prepare your own, or you can coordinate your own altar design.

Spells for Protection

In chapter 3, you learned of the protective amulets and symbols that the Egyptians believed guaranteed protection. You may choose to use any of those that appeal to you, in conjunction with the scripts given below. The numerous scripts that appear in magical papyri address the Egyptian need to be protected from sea and river beasts who posed a threat, and their need to protect the deceased from the evil god, Apep, and other threatening entities. Although it is probable that more protection spells existed, there don't appear to be further scripts addressing protection needed from another person, aside from the protective amulets.

Protective spells were written on small pieces of papyrus or linen and hung around the individual's neck, or carried. This method was also frequently used in healing magic. Spells were hung around the sick person's neck, or attached to the ailing part of the body. You can do the same with the spells below, or you can write your own spells for this purpose.

The Goddess of Protection

Auset is known as "the great goddess, the divine mother, the mistress of charms and enchantments." She is depicted in the form of a woman, with a headdress in the shape of a seat, the hieroglyph that forms her name. She sometimes wears steer horns upon her head, sometimes plumes and feathers. At times, she wears a scorpion or the star of Sothis (DogStar) on her crown. There are a few aspects of Auset that can best be learned by reading the books on mythology in the Bibliography.

Auset is a goddess of nature who saved the Sun-god Ra from a poisonous snake bite when he told her his true name. She obtained the use of the words of power from Tehuti, and is known as one of the most powerful magicians among the Egyptian deities.

Figure 11. Auset (Isis).

Auset protected Ra. Isis (see figure 11) searched out the body of her husband, Ausar, after his brother, Set, murdered him, and then erected temples to Ausar after Set had cut his body into pieces and scattered them across Egypt. Auset is the Great Mother, mother of Heru, and protector of all humans and creatures. She is armed with the greatest of magical abilities.

Many divination and magical scripts invoke Auset. Below, you will learn of Auset's amulet of protection that can be used in your practice. You may also wish to write your own protection or magical script invoking Auset, using her power for your own workings.

Below are two protective scripts. You may wish to use them in their original form or alter them slightly to meet your own needs.

A Protection Spell of the Ptolemies

At the time of the Ptolemies, people of the Graeco-Egyptian dynasties, there was a book called *The Book of Overthrowing Apep*. The evil god/monster, Apep, was considered the ultimate enemy of the god, Ra. A company of priests performed a service to free Ra from the attacks of Apep and to protect the Sun (Ra) from any corruption of weather. A portion of the book describes a spell to protect Ra from Apep, which you may use as a protection spell in shape-shifting to Ra and conquering your source of menace as Apep.

Spirit-gathering: You will need a private, dark location, solar and lunar eye symbols, or Ra and Heru figures or statues, an oil lamp (for light), lamp oil or kerosene, matches, a censer, incense (your choice), one sheet of papyrus, natural ink, and a reed pen or other pen.

Conduct this spell in as ceremonial a fashion as desired. You should be washed and ceremonially cleansed from all defilement. Privacy is a must. Dress comfortably, in Egyptian garb or in a ritual cloak. You may be naked.

You may wish to set up an altar with pictures, figures, or symbolic representations of Ra and Heru. Candles, incense, and other enhancers can be used.

1. Set up your altar. Light your incense and lamp.
2. The scribe gave instructions for the names of Apep to be written onto papyrus. Write the name(s) of your enemy on a new papyrus, or on paper.
3. After you write the name(s), the scribe states that the following spell should be recited "firmly with the mouth:"

> Down upon thy face, O Apep, enemy of Ra! The flame which cometh forth from the Eye of Heru advanceth against thee. Thou art thrust down into the flame of fire and it cometh against thee. Its flame is deadly to thy soul, and to thy spirit, and to thy words of power, and to thy body, and to thy shade. The lady of fire prevaileth over thee, the flame pierceth thy soul, it maketh an end of thy person, and it darteth into thy

form. The Eye of Heru which is powerful against its enemy hath cast thee down, it devoureth thee, the great fire trieth thee, the Eye of Ra prevaileth over thee, the flame devoureth thee, and what escapeth from it hath no being. Get thee back, for thou art cut asunder, thy soul is shriveled up, thy accursed name is buried in oblivion, and silence is upon it, and it hath fallen out of remembrance. Thou hast come to an end, thou hast been driven away, and thou art forgotten, forgotten, forgotten.

4. Burn the papyrus containing the names in the lamp flame, when Ra is rising (sunrise), at noon, or at sunset.

Many amulets were known to provide protection. Any object inscribed with the name of a deity or his or her emblem or picture became an amulet with protective powers. These powers remained active as long as the substance lasted and as long as the name, emblem, or picture, was not erased from it.[3]

Auset Tyet/Buckle Protection Spell

This spell is taken from chapter CLVI of *The Book of the Dead* and uses the buckle amulet you learned about in chapter 3. Make this amulet from modeling compound or engrave it on any object to benefit from its influence. Engrave the buckle on jewelry, or make a buckle pendant from wood, leather, or other material. Craft it to wear as it was worn upon the necks of royalty and mummies.

Spirit-gathering: You will need materials for making the tyet/buckle amulet, an oil lamp, lamp oil, matches, frankincense, and a censer.

1. Purify yourself and make your amulet in a ritual manner (see chapter 3). Assure that you have privacy and the ability to focus on this spell for greatest benefit.

---

3 E. A. Wallis Budge, *Egyptian Magic* (New York: Dover, 1971), p. 65

2. Once your buckle is prepared, hold it, as you stand in a lamp-lit room, with frankincense burning, and recite the following spell:

   > The blood of Auset, and the strength of Auset, and the words of power of Auset shall be mighty to act as powers to protect this great and divine being, and to guard him from him/her that would do unto him anything that he holdeth in abomination.

Recite the spell as given, even if what you seek is protection for yourself or another individual.

Spells for Acquiring Praise

The Egyptians used magic to accomplish self-serving desires and goals in daily life. The ego was not considered a negative part of existence, but rather an important factor that should be enhanced and exercised.

While magic was used for healing and benefiting other individuals, the magician did not hesitate to use magic for the most trivial matters, including for purposes of appearing great and honorable in the eyes of other people. This is no different than how we, as individuals, like to present ourselves today. Each of us hopes that we are looked upon favorably in the eyes of our parents, teachers, employers, friends, and the outer world. No one likes to be slandered or considered an "outsider" in cliques. It is interesting to consider how much in common our social goals have with those of ancient Egyptians and how little the human race has changed in its social behavior over the centuries.

The God in Spells for Acquiring Praise

Tehuti is summoned in many spells for gaining favor and praise (see figure 12, page 171). This may stem from his mythological deed of restoring the Eye of Heru, which

Figure 12. Tehuti (Thoth).

enabled Heru to conquer Set and be crowned king. As the god of truth and right, Tehuti acted as judge in the battles between Heru and Set. He gave Heru his favor. This may be the reason he was chosen for spells to obtain favor.

Below are two spells for acquiring praise and favor, taken from *The Leyden Papyrus* (Col Xl).

An Ape of Wax Spell

Under the divine intelligence of Tehuti, the world was created by a word. Eight elements, four male and four female, arose out of primeval Nu, or "One," which possessed both male and female qualities. These eight elements were depicted as four apes, who stand in adoration and sing hymns of praise to the rising Sun. The ape represents "the first life" into which the magician shapeshifts his ka/double for the purpose of approaching the invoked Tehuti.

Tehuti was a lunar god who was represented by a baboon, his alter ego. Ancient magicians were clever enough to choose to appear, not only as a relative to the baboon, but as one of Tehuti's greatest creations, in order to request favors from him.

Spirit-gathering: You will need a short, fat wax candle or lump of wax, a knife to carve the wax. You may refer to chapter 4 for instructions in shape-shifting.

Arrange your altar in a private room or an area outdoors. You may choose to burn incense and decorate your sacred space to enhance it. Avoid interruption during this spell. Dress comfortably. Tight clothing can hinder your ability to concentrate and shape-shift into the ape form.

1. In preparation, use a knife to carve your candle or lump of wax into the shape of an ape. The shape does not have to be perfect.
2. Stand or sit before your altar. Look at the waxen ape figure momentarily, then close your eyes and visualize it in your mind's eye. Concentrate. When you have the figure clearly visualized, project your double body into it, then recite the following script:

    Come to me, O . . . thy beautiful name. O Tehuti, hasten, hasten; come to me. Let me see thy beautiful face here today . . . I stand being in the form of an ape; and do thou greet me with praise and adoration with thy tongue . . . come unto me that thou mayest hearken to my voice today, and mayest save me from all things evil and all slander. Ho! thou whose form is of his great and mysterious form, from whose begetting came forth a god, who resteth deep in Thebes; I am of the great Lady, under whom cometh forth the Nile, I am the face of reverence great . . . soul in his protection; I am the noble child who is in the House of Ra: I am the noble dwarf who is in the cavern . . . the ibis as a true protection, who resteth in On; I am the master of the great foe, lord of obstructer of semen, mighty . . . my name, I am a ram, son of a ram, Sarpot Mui-Sro and vice versa is my name, Light-scarab-noble is my true name, Light-scarab-noble is my true name, grant me praise and love and reverence from _____ (name who you seek it from) today, and let him/her grant me all good things, and let him/her give me nourishment and fat things, and let him/her do for me everything which I wish for; and let him/her not inure me so as to do me harm, nor let him/her say to me a thing which I hate, today, tonight, this month, this year, this hour . . . But as for my enemies, the Sun shall impede their hearts and blind their eyes, and cause the darkness to be in their faces; for I am Birai . . . rai, depart ye, Rai; I am the son of Sochmet, I am Bikt, bull of Lat, I am Gat, son of Gat, who is in the Underworld, who rests deep in the Great Residence in On, I am son of Hek-net, lady of the protecting bandage, who binds them with thongs . . . I am the phallus which the great and mighty Powers guard, which rests in Bubastis; I am the divine shrewmouse which resteth within Skhym; lord of Ay, sole lord . . . is my name Light-scarab-noble is my true name, Light-scarab-noble is my true name. Ho! all ye these gods, whose names I have spoken here today, come to me, that ye may harken to that which I have said today and rescue me from all weakness, every disgrace, everything, every evil today; grant me praise, love and reverence before such an one, the King and his host, the desert and its animals; let him/ her do everything which I shall say to him/her together with every man who shall see me or to whom I shall speak or who shall speak to me, among every man, every woman, every child, every old man, every person or animal or thing in the whole land, which shall see me in these moments today, and let them cause my praise to be in their hearts of everything which I shall do daily, together with those who shall come to me, to overthrow every enemy, hasten, hasten, quickly, quickly, before I say them or repeat them.

The wax ape has been charged. The magic is done. The wax figure may be carried with you, or placed somewhere in your home.

In this spell, the "House of Ra" refers to the place "Heliopolis." "The ibis as a true protection," represents Tehuti. In fact, Tehuti's head is that of an ibis upon a human, male body. "Son of Sochmet" may refer to Mihos, or Nefer-tem, who are lion gods. "The Great Residence in On," is the name of the temple of the Sun at Heliopolis.[4]

The shrew-mouse was sacred to the blind Heru in the town of Letoplis. In medicine-magic, the shrew-mouse was used to produce blindness or death in a man, and erotic arousal in a woman. "Skhym" and "Ay" are both names of Letopolis in the delta.[5]

Wreath Spell

Use the spell script described above to recite over the wreath of flowers used below.

Spirit-gathering: The original spirit-gathering for this spell is incomplete as translated from the papyrus. The materials needed are supposedly a fish, oil of lilies, styrax, prime frankincense, and the seeds of the "great-of-love" plant. All of these ingredients are to be mixed together in a metal vase. Since the ingredients are not clearly translated or practical, it is best to decide on a mixture of materials you feel is appropriate. The purpose of the concoction is to anoint a wreath and yourself. You can choose to use essential oils known in Egypt in place of the above. In addition, you will need a wreath of flowers, or materials to make an organic wreath, a mixture as described above, or Egyptian oils, and a metal vase to hold the mixture or oils.

---

4 F. L. Griffith and Herbert Thompson, eds., *The Leyden Papyrus: An Egyptian Magical Book* (New York: Dover, 1974), p. 83.

5 F. L. Griffith and Herbert Thompson, eds., *The Leyden Papyrus*, p. 84.

1. Make a wreath of flowers and anoint the wreath with the mixed oil.
2. Recite the script given above over the wreath seven times before the Sun rises in the morning and before speaking to any man.
3. After reciting the script, extract the oil from the metal vase and anoint your face with it.
4. Place the wreath in your hand and proceed to any place where you can be among people. The wreath will bring you great praise among them.

Spells for Averting Anger

Throughout history, people have at times found themselves at odds with an employer, an elder, or an authority figure. The anxiety each of us feels when we have a dispute with an authority figure can be overwhelming. Calmly discussing the matter with that authority figure, or apologizing for a wrongful action, usually yields the best results. The Egyptian magician, however, did not want to take any chances. Magic was essential to gaining a better position with someone in authority, even if the matter was trivial.

No deity had the duty to avert anger. As you will learn below, magicians tried both negotiation and threats to achieve this goal. The following spell is taken from *The Leyden Papyrus* (Col. XV). It is not known from the translation if the spell was actually intended to improve communications with a king, sovereign, superior officer, or employer. It can probably be used with any authority figure in mind.

Spirit-gathering: Upon rising in the morning, ritually bathe and prepare yourself for the day. There are no specific preparation instructions provided.

1. The scribe states that this spell is conducted before going to meet with the superior who fights and will not parley with you.

2. Recite the following spell seven times:

    Do not pursue me, thou! I am Papipetou Metoubanes. I am carrying the mummy of Ausar and I am proceeding to take it to Abydos, to take it to Tastai, and to deposit it in Alkhai; if _____ (insert superior's name) deal blows at me, I will cast it at him/her.

3. Alternatively you can recite this script seven times:

    Do not pursue me, _____ (superior's name), I am Papipetu Metubanes. I am carrying the mummy of Ausar, I am proceeding to take it to Abydos, to cause it to rest in Alkhah. If _____ (superior's name) fight with me today, I will cast it away.

Certainly it would be a terrible thing to throw away Ausar's mummy. The intention is that the superior will not argue, wishing to preserve the mummy, and that the gods will grant your desire so you do not harm Ausar's mummy.

The city of Abydos mentioned in the spell was the cult-center of Ausar in ancient Egypt. "Papipetu Metubanes" is thought to be a magical name, possibly meaning "I am the servant of him that is great."

Spells for Acquiring Success

You may have a goal, project, or situation in your life that could use magical influence to assure achievement. The following success spell was used for numerous challenges, including asking someone out for a date or succeeding at a career goal. The spell was used for both trivial or crucial matters that would benefit the magician.

The God in Spells for Acquiring Success

The following spell invokes Phre, who is a form of the Sun-god, Ra. (See figure 13, page 171.) As the Sun fol-

Figure 13. Ra (Phre).

lowed its daily course, it vanquished night and darkness, succeeding over the forces of chaos. The Egyptians invented a moral conception of the Sun that represented the triumph of truth and right over falsehood and wrongdoing.

The morning and midday Sun promised Phre's highest power in working magic to acquire success. The Egyptians believed the Sun traveled in a boat to the Underworld at night, battling to maintain order. The sunrise each day gave prima facia proof of its success.

A Spell with an Invocation of Phre

The following spell can be found in *The Leyden Papyrus* (Col. XVI).

Spirit-gathering: Rise early in the morning on the day you will work the spell. This guarantees that everything you will do that day will prosper. It is important that you conduct the spell immediately upon rising, before speaking to anyone or doing anything else. This also assures that you are free from every abomination.

Go to a window in your house, or venture outdoors, so that you face Phre, the Sun. Pronounce this invocation before Phre three times, or seven times for best result. As you recite, visualize in your mind's eye that what you desire has been achieved. In other words, see your final success, not what may lead to your success. Do not allow any worries or thoughts of failure to enter your mind. Before you begin, you may wish to take a few moments to clear your mind and concentrate. Then speak these words:

> Io, Tabao, Sokhom-moa, Okh-okh-khan-bouzanau, Aniesi, Ekomphtho, Ketho, Sethouri, Thmila, Alouapokhri, let everything that I shall apply my hand to here today, let it happen.

Another invocation given in *The Leyden Papyrus* (Col. XVII) serves the same purpose. Prepare in the same manner as above, then recite the script three or seven times:

> Iotabao, Sokh-ommoa, Okh-okh-khan, Bouzanau, Aniesi, Ekomphtho, Ketho, Sethori, Thmilaalouapokhri may everything succeed that I shall do today.

The scribe wrote the following note: "its chief matter is purity, and they will succeed." This means that your purity at the time of reciting the spell is most important to ensure its success.

Defensive Magic

Egyptian magicians were quite intolerant of their enemies. No compassion was allowed for enemies. The most severe forms of "negative magic" were used to silence enemies or to succeed against them. This fact is one that separates Egyptian magic from contemporary "white magic."

There were many ways a magician could conquer an enemy. Attempting to trick the enemy into thinking he had attacked the wrong person was one of them. If it was thought that the enemy had worked negative magic or sent a hostile spirit, like a demon, to cause harm, the magician might shape-shift into the form of a powerful deity and evoke the demon. Once the demon was present, the magician, in god-form, might convince the demon it was attacking a mighty deity instead of the targeted individual. The magician hoped that this trickery would frighten the demon into leaving. Another course of action for dealing with unsavory creatures sent by an enemy was to persuade the menace to leave with promises of reward.

Blotting out the name of an individual assured his eradication. Writing the name on papyrus, then simply blotting it out with ink was a popular method. An individual whose name was in any way tainted or destroyed was assured misfortune.

"Sealing" was another method to restrain an enemy. Images and pictures of enemies drawn on papyrus were placed in sealed boxes to restrain them from harming or succeeding over the magician. Another method, based on the same ideology, was to bind an enemy with knot magic. Both methods can easily be incorporated into any existing ancient script, or one that you create yourself.

In cursing ceremonies, execration texts were written onto red pots, which were somehow broken as a symbolic gesture of destroying the enemy's power.

A God for Defeating Enemies

Set has always had two characteristics—one good and one malevolent. He constantly battled with Heru, his opposite. Heru represented daylight and order, and Set represented the night and chaos. For the Egyptians, this symbolized the battle between right and wrong (see figure 14, page 180).

Figure 14. Set (Seth).

Set's true name (and nature) is "the evil day on which nothing can be conceived or born."[6] It was not until the later phases of Egyptian culture that Set was considered intrinsically evil. In earlier Egyptian mythology, Set defended Ra against his most threatening enemy, the serpent god, Apep. Set's cunning and chaotic aspects, coupled with his devotion to defending fellow deities in need, makes him the ideal god for defensive magic. He is a suitable fighter for a magician who wishes to "fight fire with fire."

An Egyptian magician might have also invoked Set to harness his power to overcome or control antagonistic entities evoked during magical work. Set was also invoked in his form of a griffin in many spells found in magical papyri. The Greeks called him "Typhon" in recognition of his personification of evil. In Greek mythology, Typhon, the child of Mother Earth

[6] Geraldine Pinch, *Magic in Ancient Egypt*, p. 32.

and Tartarus (the place of torture in Hades), was the largest monster ever born.[7] Typhon rests beneath Mount Etna in Sicily, the myth concludes, where today he explodes with molten rock and fire from within the volcano. He was a god of violence and chaos. The color red was attributed to him.

Obviously, Set, or "Typhon," should be invoked with great care, as his fierce power can be quite harmful. If you are protecting yourself from, or battling against, evil magic or intent that someone has worked against you, then such power can be necessary and beneficial.

Invocation of Set (To Succeed Over an Enemy)

This script is an excerpt from *The Leyden Papyrus* (Col. XXIII). There is an original spirit-gathering that accompanies the script, however, that is neither suitable or practical, involving, for example, acquiring a set-stone of Syria, which is very difficult. The script alone, however, can serve us well.

The translators of *The Leyden Papyrus* have noted that the spell seems to inflict ague and fever in the line below that reads "strike down him or her with frost and fire." Ague describes the regular, recurring chills that accompany a high fever. As such, this spell can be considered as working magic to make your enemy physically ill, or you can use it for defeating your enemy through psychic warfare. It is meant to defeat any attempts an enemy might make to psychically, mentally, or psychologically attack you. You could, however, change the meaning of "frost and fire" to apply to unworldly psychic attacks.

Spirit-gathering (revised): As this is an outdoor spell, it may be difficult for you to perform the magic in public view wearing Egyptian or magical regalia, so casual

---

7 Barbara Watterson, *Gods of Ancient Egypt* (New York: Facts on File, 1988), p. 116.

clothing is acceptable. The invocation of Set should be recited before the full Sun, in the morning:

> I invoke thee who art in the void air, terrible, invisible, almighty, god of gods, dealing destruction and making desolate, O thou that hatest a household well established. When thou wast cast out of Egypt and out of the country thou wast entitled, "He that destroyeth all and is unconquered." I invoke thee, Typhon Set, I perform thy ceremonies of divination, for I invoke thee by thy powerful name in words which thou canst not ref use to hear: Io erbeth, Iopakerbeth, Iobolkhoseth, Iopatathnax, Iosoro, Ioneboutosoualeth, Aktiophi, Ereskhigal, Neboposoaleth, Aberamenthoou, Lerthexanax, Ethreluoth, Nemareba, Aemina, entirely come to me and approach and strike down him or her (your menace) with frost and fire; he has wronged me, and has poured out the blood of Typhon beside him or her: therefore I do these things.

Love Spells

Spells to acquire the love and affection of another were widely used. Unlike modern love magic, Egyptian magicians sometimes used severe measures to have those whom they desired, even cursing the person's current lover or spouse, and wishing them dead. Most love spells, however, spoke beautiful words of power from the heart.

The main emphasis of most Egyptian love spells is to remove the persons desired from their house, so that the magician can covet and court them. The infatuated magus wanted assurance that his or her object of love had not a moment of peace or sleep, and that the person's entire life would be interrupted, so that courting that person would be easier.

There are numerous Egyptian love spells. Most are written for male magicians attempting to win the affec-

Figure 15. Het-heru (Hathor).

tions of a woman. To maintain the integrity of the ancient scripts, gender elements have not been changed here. We know that priestess-magicians also used love spells and that female magi should not shy away from using them.

A Goddess of Love Magic

Het-heru is the goddess of love, fertility, beauty, and Utopia. She was the Mistress of Maidens who provided husbands to women who adored her (see figure 15). She was particularly revered by unmarried women, for she charmed their metallic mirrors and protective eyeliners made of malachite, and helped them maintain their beauty. Love-struck men and women wrote poems to her in the hope that she would reward them with their beloved. Prayer and offerings were also made to gain her favor. When performing the spells below, you may wish to make an offering to Het-heru to capture her power for your magic. These two spells from *The Leyden Papyrus,* and one from Budge's *Egyptian Magic,* are simple and effective.

A Love Spell Using a Lamp and Figures

(*The Leyden Papyrus,* Verso Col. XVI)

Spirit-gathering: You will need myrrh or natural ink, a reed pen or writing utensil, a clean linen wick, an oil lamp, lamp oil or kerosene, matches, a hair of your beloved, and the following figures (made of wax or other materials, or drawn on papyrus): three scarabs, three hawks, and three goats.

1. Prepare your sacred, magical space as preferred. Line up the figures to stand before you, with the lamp on an altar or table.
2. Charge the figures with the script below. Concentrate on your intent and visualize your desires fulfilled.
3. Write the following script in myrrh ink (or any natural ink) on the linen wick:

   Armioout, Sithani, Outhani, Aryamnoi, Sobrtat, Birbat, Misirythat, Amsie-tharmithat: bring _____ (the person's name) daughter of (her/his parents' name) out of her abodes in which she is, to any house and any place which_____ (your name, or the person you work the magic for), son of _____ (parents' name) is in; she loving him and craving for him, she making the gift of his desire at every moment.

4. Recite the script seven times aloud over the figures and strongly visualize your magic accomplished.
5. Burn the wick safely in your house from evening until morning.

A Spell Using Love Figures

This spell was written by Pindar in *Pythia* (iv. 213). Pindar was a Graeco-Roman writer who lived in the first half of the fifth century before Christ.[8] Pindar learned the use of wax figures in magic from Egypt, which is why it is of interest to us. E. A. Wallis Budge, in his book *Egyptian Magic,* received this spell from F. G. Kenyon of the British Museum.

Spirit-gathering: You will need wax, mixed with pitch and gum, to make a dog figure about eight fingers long, an altar or table, a tablet or journal, natural ink, a reed pen or writing utensil, and a tripod (a photography tripod will do).

1. To secure the favors of a lover, engrave certain words of power over the dog's ribs. (Unfortunately, we are not given the words to write. Choose words of love and desire, or an invocation to Het-heru.)
2. Write on a tablet other words of power, or the names of the beings that possess magical powers that you wish to use.
3. Place the figure of the dog on top of the tablet, and place the tablet atop the tripod.
4. You, or the person for whom you work the magic, must recite the words of power which have been written on the dog's ribs and on the tablet.
5. Two things can happen: Either the dog will snap or snarl at the inquirer, or he will bark. If the dog snarls and snaps, the inquirer will not gain his or her desired end. If the dog barks, the lover will come and be receptive to affection.

A Spell of Separation

(*The Leyden Papyrus*, Col. XIII)

If a person is married, a separation spell is necessary so that the seeker may properly and effectively pursue the individual of desire.

---

[8] E. A. Wallis Budge, *Egyptian Magic,* pp. 96, 97.

Figure 16. Seb (Geb).

Spirit-gathering: The spirit-gathering is incomplete in the original script, due to illegible writing on the papyrus. It is clear, however, that you will need a wax or drawn figure of the god Seb, holding a uas-scepter, and an altar or table. Seb represents the Earth god. The illustration above depicts Seb as he appears in many Egyptian wall portraits, in his human form, wearing a crown and with a scepter in his right hand (see figure 16).

Lay the figure or picture of Seb on your altar or table. Recite the following script over the depicted Seb. As you do, visualize your purpose and goal achieved.

> Woe! Woe! Flame! Flame! Seb assumed his form of a bull, coivit matris suane Tefnet, again . . . because the heart of his father cursed his face; the fury of him whose soul is as flame, while his body is as a pillar, so that he fills the earth with flame and the mountains shoot with tongues—the fury of every god and goddess Ankh-uer. Lalat, Bareshak, Belkesh, be

> cat upon _____ (the woman's husband, in this case) the son of _____ (husband's parents' name) and _____ (woman's name) the daughter of ____ (woman's parents' name), send the fire toward his heart and the flame in his place of sleeping, fire of hatred never ceasing to enter into his heart at any time, until he cast _____ (the woman) daughter of _____ (her parents' name) out of his abode, she having hatred to his heart, she having quarrel to his face; grant for him the nagging and squabbling, the fighting and quarreling between them at all times, until they are separated from each other, without agreeing again forever.

The figure of Seb is charged. Leave it on your altar or, if drawn on paper, wear or carry it.

A Love Spell Using Pottery

Below is a love spell written by a woman who lived in the New Kingdom of Egypt. She placed the poem upon a vase. It demonstrates poetry used as a vehicle for magical script that possibly was written to Het-heru so the woman could acquire the man she admired.

The woman, described as dressed in royal linen, was probably a priestess or a member of a royal family. The fish depicted in the poem was a phallic symbol in ancient Egypt. This is the most erotic love poem written by an Egyptian woman that has survived for our review:

> I love to go and bathe before you.
> I allow you to see my beauty
> in a dress of royal linen, drenched with camphor. . . .
> I go down into the water
> to be with you
> and come up to you again
> with a red fish,
> looking splendid on my fingers.

I place it before you . . . .
Come! Look at me![9]

You may choose to use a poetic style for your magical scripts. It is an especially nice touch when designing love spells.

Sex Magic

This form of magic allowed magicians to seduce and acquire the individual they desired. Unlike contemporary spells that use sex to work magic, the Egyptians used magic to improve performance in sex.

There was no god or goddess of sex in Egyptian mythology. Set was well-known for his lust and unrestrained sexual practices, however. Since Set was bisexual and ruled all common and unusual sexual desires, however, he is an appropriate god to invoke for sex magic.

In a sense, the magical techniques used in these spells was not magic at all, but consisted of recipes for love potions, stimulants, and oils that were applied to the sex organs to assure optimum performance. If the recipes worked, on the other hand, magical experience certainly took place for the recipient and the magician appeared capable of fantastic sexual acts.

Despite vigorous research, the only erotic spells that have been found are those intended to be used by a man to procure a woman. Moreover, most of the recipes of Egyptian erotic magic are not practical for use today. Some ingredients are bizarre and repulsive—the dung of a crocodile and the gall of a male goat. When mixed with other ingredients these produced an ointment to anoint the penis to increase the woman's pleasure. The two spells selected here use ingredients that can be obtained today. These spells offer an authentic glimpse into Egyptian erotic magic.

9 Cairo vase. 1266 + 25218.

Acacia and Honey Spell

This spell for making a woman love a man can be found in *The Leyden Papyrus* (Verso Col. Ill).

The acacia is a thorny tree or shrub of the mimosa family. It is sometimes called the locust tree. Some types provide gum arabic or dyes. The juice of its fruit, or sap, is the ingredient called for in this spell.

Spirit-gathering: You will need acacia fruit or sap, and some natural honey

1. Grind the acacia pods with the honey. Mix thoroughly.
2. The man anoints his phallus with the mixture, and then lies with the woman.

Stallion Ointment Spell

The scribe who recorded this spell writes: "The foam from a stallion's mouth is certain to make a woman *amare coitum suum*. She will orgasm. The man is to anoint his phallus with it and lie with the woman."[10]

Healing Magic

The Egyptians may have been the first to use holistic and herbal medicine. Some papyri contain a type of dictionary for identifying plants, minerals, and spices, giving their names and definitions, along with instructions for their use. Healing of fever, insect stings, a bone caught in the throat, gout, water in an ear, and hemorrhage in a woman are but a few health concerns for which the Egyptians had treatments.

Egyptian medicine was used with equal frequency for both positive and negative purposes. Under the doctrines of medicine, potions and extracts from plants were offered to ensure a quick death to, or at the least the maiming of, an enemy. Drugging someone for a self-serving purpose

[10] F. L. Griffith and Herbert Thompson, eds., *The Leyden Papyrus*, p. 187.

was also common, a practice which is no different from placing a disabling drug in someone's drink at a rambunctious party today.

Egyptian magicians and physicians practiced gynecology. A pregnancy test using a plant existed in ancient Egypt. Treating yeast infections and other ailments suffered by women was common practice. Women received very good care.

What is considered "new" in holistic and herbal practice today is not really new. These forms of medicine have been practiced since the existence of humanity. Contemporary scientists and physicians consider both these forms of treatment "new" simply because synthetic chemicals and drugs have been produced, and the technology of modern medicine has allowed us to evolve beyond the exclusive use of organic materials for healing.

The medical technology and synthetic drugs used today would not exist without the basic foundation of holistic and herbal medicine of the ancient civilizations. If our world suffered a man-made or natural catastrophe, our modern conveniences and resources for medical treatment would all disappear. It is best to learn and practice all types of medicine, past and present, to be prepared.

A God and Goddess of Healing

The Moon god, Khonsu, was famed as a god of healing, according to a stele found in his temple at Thebes. He is depicted as a young, mummified man holding a crook, flail, and a waas-scepter in his hands. He also wears a single side-lock of hair, a style typical of Egyptian youth (see figure 17, page 191). Khonsu can be helpful to you in healing magic and divination by the Moon. (To learn more, see the Gods and Godesses Glossary page, 201.) Sekhmet is the renowned lion-goddess who has the body of a female human and the head of a female lion

Figure 17. Khonsu.

(see figure 18, page 192). She is both a bloodthirsty mistress of war and a goddess of healing. She can kill or cure. Her priests were entrusted with the task of exorcising the demons which were believed to be the cause of many illnesses. Who better to fight and conquer illness than the mistress of war?

Both these deities can be useful in using your healing scripts. Khonsu seems best suited for healing magic that uses the influence of lunar phases. He can be used for general healing purposes. Sekhmet is ideal to use when working magic to banish a virus, cancer cells, or any harmful toxin in the body. Combining her healing qualities with those of warfare, you can absorb those qualities and project them through your energy in healing. This may stimulate the immune system and help it fight off the invasion.

Below, several healing spells are provided from *The Leyden Papyrus* that you can use.

Figure 18. Sekhmet.

To Cure Water in an Ear (Verso Col. IV): Take some salt and heat it with good wine. Clean out the ear canal carefully. Apply the mixture to the ear once a day for four days.

To Cure a Wound (Verso Col. IV): Use an herb called "ram's horn," which is in the family of the wild fennel bush. Its leaf and its stem are incised, and its seed is twisted. Pound the leaf and stem when they are dry, making them into a dry powder. Apply the powder to any wound and the wound will be cured.

To Cure Water in a Woman (Verso Col. VI): Take a dish and place a cup of old sweet wine in it, then add some fresh rue. Soak from dawn until midday. The woman should bathe and then drink the wine. When it is evening, dip a rag or bandage in genuine honey and put it on the woman until morning. Repeat this for three or four days.

A Remedy for Gout (Verso Col. VIII): Take an ant and cook it in the oil of henna. Anoint the feet with it. When you have finished, take Alexandrian figs, dried grapes, and potentilla and pound them with wine. Anoint the feet with this mixture then blow on the person with your mouth.

A Talisman for Gout (Verso Col. X): Conduct this spell when the Moon is in the constellation of Leo. Write the following on a strip of silver or tin:

> **δέρμα έηαφιον, 'θεμβαραθεμ, ονρεμβρενουτιπε, αιοχθον, σεμ-μαραθεμμον, ναιοου**

Place the strip on a deer skin and bind it to the foot. Then recite this script:

> Let _____ (affected person's name) son/daughter of _____ (parents' name) recover from every pain which is in his/her feet and two legs.

A Remedy for a Sprained Foot (Verso Col. XI): Very excellent. You wash the foot with the juice of a cucumber. Rub it well onto the foot.

A Spell to Heal Opthalmia (Verso Col. XX): Ophthalmia is a severe inflammation of the eye(s), such as conjunctivitis. You will need a new sheet of papyrus, writing ink, a reed pen, vegetable oil, salt, and nasturtium seed.

Mix the oil, salt and nasturtium seed together, and say this script to charge it:

> Ho! Amon, this lofty male, this male of Ethiopia, who came down from Meroe to Egypt, he finds my son Heru betaking himself as fast as his feet move, and he injured his head with three spells in Ethiopian language, and he finds _____ (ailing person's name) son/daughter of _____ (parents' name), and carries him as fast as his feet move, and he injures his head with three spells in Ethiopia n language: Gentini, Tentina, Kwkwby, Akkhe, Akha.

Anoint the ailing person with the mixture. Then write the above script and draw an eye with rays projecting from it (the papyrus does not specify which eye) on a papyrus sheet. Use this as a written amulet and tie it to the sick person's body. Charge it by saying: "Thou art this eye of heaven."

A Spell Spoken to a Dog Bite (Col. XIX): Pound garlic with fine meal and put it on the dog bite. Address it daily until it is healed, speaking to it the following script:

> I have come forth from Arkhah, my mouth being full of blood of a black dog. I spit it out. O this dog, who is among the ten dogs which belong to Anpu, the son of his body, extract thy venom, remove thy saliva from me. If thou dost not extract thy venom and remove thy saliva, I will take thee up to the court of the temple of Ausar, my watchtower. I will do for thee the parapage of birds like the voice of Auset, the sorceress, the mistress of sorcery, who bewitches everything and is not bewitched in her name of Auset the sorceress.

A similar spell suggests pounding rue with honey and applying this to the dog bite, then giving the affected person a cup of water to drink.

A Spell to Cure Fever (Verso Col. XXXIII): This script was difficult to translate. In some areas, it may be difficult to understand. Say this script initially (the first couple of times) over vegetable or essential Egyptian oil. Then, anoint the sick person's hands, body, and feet, and pronounce the words to him/her. Recite the script seven times:

> Heru . . . he was going up a hill at midday in the verdure season, mounted on a white horse . . . on a black horse were the papyrus rolls being on him, those of the Great of Five in his besom. He found all the gods seated at the place of judgment—eating of the produce of the Nile. "My Chief," said they, "Heru, come, art thou eating? Heru, come, wilt thou eat?" He said, "Take yourselves from me; there is no desire in me for eating. I am ill in my head; I am ill in my body; a fe-

> ver hath taken hold of me, a South wind hath seized me." Doth Isis cease to make magic? Doth Nebt-het cease to give health? Are the sixteen Netbeou, is the one Power of God, are the 365 gods seated to eat the produce of the fields of the Nile, my Chief, until they remove the fever from the head of the son of Isis and from the head of _____ (sick person's name) son/ daughter of _____ (parents' name), the fevers by night, the fevers by day, the headache, this burning, this heat of the fevers . . . of his feet, remove from the head of _____ (sick person's name) son/daughter of _____ (parents' name).

"Are the sixteen Netbeou," could refer to the sixteen cubits of the Nile, or the body of Ausar that was torn into sixteen pieces.[11] The 365 gods indicate one god for each day of the year.

Egyptian Evocation Techniques

An evocation is a command to an unworldly spirit or hostile god to appear and work as instructed by the magician. They were common practice in Egypt and are still used today in ceremonial magic and sorcery.

Evocation differs from the invocation of gods. During invocation, gods and spirits are invited to be present by using their name, and by visual and sensory perceptions associated with the specific being's summons. Spirits and gods are invoked to give protection to the magician and lend power for the magical work at hand.

Unlike contemporary magic practice, Egyptian magic did not involve casting a circle or triangle of protection. Preparation for evocation included the necessity of being pure, dressing in a magical cloak or ceremonial garments, and gathering any needed

---

[11] F. L. Griffith and Herbert Thompson, eds., *The Leyden Papyrus*, p. 204.

ritual tools. Confident of their power, Egyptian sorcerers used only words spoken in a commanding voice, gestures, and ritual tools to evoke a spirit or god to do their bidding.

Visualization, concentration, and the use of the energy of the evoked being will make your magic a success. When evoking spirits or hostile gods, you are harnessing another form of energy to amplify your own into the cosmos. Eventually, that energy will manifest on the physical plane to cause change.

As the following spells do not have specific instructions for use provided by the papyrus, you may employ these spells in custom-made evocations and rituals.

Protective Amulet Spells

Graeco-Egyptian papyri provide instructions for the use of amulets in preparation for evocation to protect and empower you. This short amuletic spell also works f or invoking a feisty deity, such as the goddess Sekhmet. The subsequent spells are all taken from *The Leyden Papyrus*.

Spirit-gathering: You will need water, a magical statue of a favorite deity, a small piece of linen, natural ink, a reed pen or writing utensil, a long-lasting herb (the papyrus does not specify), and a foot-long linen thread (the "thread of Anpu").

1. Pour water over a magical statue or figure that you frequently employ in magic.
2. Soak a piece of linen in the water and write a script on it which identifies you as the god Heru.
3. Take a long-lasting herb and roll the linen cloth around it.
4. Secure this roll with the thread of Anpu, tied seven times.
5. Wear this amulet around your neck during any rite that involves evocation of a fierce deity or being.

To Bring in a Drowned Man (Col. III): To evoke the spirit of a drowned man to do your work, place a crab or a crayfish upon a lit brazier and choose words of power to evoke him.

To Bring in a Living Man (Col. III): It is uncertain if this evocation was meant to bring the double body of a living man, an actual living man, or cause an actual living man somewhere to carry out your work via telepathy. My research indicates that the double body of a living man is correct. To bring in the double of a living man, put sulphate of copper on a lit brazier, choose words of power to recite, and then he will come in.

To Bring in a Thief (Col. III): If you wish a thief to do your bidding, put crocus powder with alum on a lit brazier.

To Dismiss Evoked Spirits, Beings and Deities (Col. III): The charm which you pronounce when you dismiss evoked spirits is: "Good dispatch, joyful dispatch!"

Knot Magic

In Egypt, knots were tied in cords for certain love spells, and for divination and evocation. In love spells, a cord of knots was usually tied upon the man (commonly his arm), before he made love to a woman to assist in making her love him. Some love spells called for a real scarab to be tied into a knot and placed upon the man. In divination and evocation, the knots sometimes represented the binding of a specific individual to control him/her, or to be able to bind the person for detection during scrying.

The excerpt below, from *The Leyden Papyrus* (Col. IX) vessel divination, demonstrates how a magician used knots to bind the spirits of the dead to him through evocation. In divination, it also served to ensure they answered his inquiries truthfully.

The entire spell is not presented here because its spirit-gathering consists of impractical items. The script is extremely long and uses a child medium. For our purpose, you only need to understand how knot magic was used and the typical words of power spoken. You can add the technique to the ancient spells above, or to your own spells.

> I am Auset and I will bind him, I am Ausar and I will bind him, I am Ausar and I will bind him . . . Lesmatot, protect me, heal me, give me love, praise and reverence in my vessel, my bandage,[12] here today.

Later, in the same spell:

> They shall rise, they shall flourish at the mouths of my vessel, my bandage, my word-seeking. Arouse them for me, me, the spirits, the dead; rouse their souls and forms at the mouth of my vessel; rouse them for me with the dead; rouse them for me, me, rouse their souls and their forms.

In the second excerpt, the magician hopes to arouse the spirits of the dead and catch them in his vessel and/or knotted cord for use.

It is unfortunate that we do not have more detailed magical instruction from ancient Egypt. Conquerors of Egypt and the early Christians destroyed much literature from Egypt's royal and temple libraries.

There are rumors that, locked away inside the Vatican in Rome, are ancient writings of spirituality and magic from Egypt and other ancient civilizations. And who knows what may be unearthed in the continued archeological excavations of new-found Egyptian tombs?

---

[12] "Bandage" is actually a cord of knots used during magic. The translators state that the Egyptian word used to name this is difficult to understand and translate; therefore, bandage was chosen.

Perhaps as time continues, we may be presented with more facts and useful information.

May the factual information within this book benefit your knowledge and practice of magic. You alone can bring the essence and power of ancient Egyptian magic to our modern world. Keep alive the roots and traditions of Egypt that helped form the magical systems of our modern day.

Glossary of Egyptian Gods and Goddesses

The following glossary provides a practical guide to understanding the Egyptian deities discussed in this book. The Greek or English names given to the Egyptian deities, as well as their definitions, are included.

Abrasax (Abraxas): A Sun/creator god who appears in Gnostic gems and was worshiped as having magical power of the highest class. His name is invincible. There is a difference of opinion as to his name's meaning. He is depicted as having two bodies: a man's and a bird's. Four wings extend from the bodies. From each knee projects a serpent. He has two pairs of arms and hands; one of which extends along the wings, with each hand holding symbols of life, power, stability, along with two knives and two serpents. The other pair is pendent, with the right hand holding the sign of life and the other holding a scepter. His face is that of a hideous old man. He wears a pylon-shaped crown on his head with several symbols of fire on each side. On the crown are figures of animals and above it is a pair of horns that support eight knives and the figure of a god with his arms raised, typifying "millions of years."

Amun: An air god, he is the husband of the mother-goddess, Mut. His name means "Invisible One." Considered a mysterious god, his statues within shrines were shrouded by custom. He is a god known for his virility and pugnacity. A goose and a ram with down-turned horns were his symbols, but he was depicted as a human man wearing a cap surmounted with two plumes and a Sun disk.

Anpu (Anubis): The son of Ausar or Ra, and the son of Auset or Nebt-het. He is depicted in either human form with a jackal's head, or as a jackal. Anpu is a god of the funeral chamber, and assists in mummification after death. At Judgment, he guards and weighs the heart against the feather of Maat on the balance. In magic, Anpu guards all magical secrets. Whole battalions of messenger demons are under his command.[1]

Apep (Apophis): A great serpent god that is the most dangerous enemy of Ra. He can take the form of a crocodile or a dragon. In Judgment scenes in funerary papyri, he is a hybrid monster formed of a hippopotamus's hind quarters, a lion's torso, and a crocodile's head. He is symbolic of any enemy, rebellion, or chaotic force in magic. Magicians used scripts that portrayed the war between Apep and Ra in the cosmos in order to conquer enemies on Earth. In some magical work, Apep was invoked against enemies.

Ausar (Osiris): Son of Seb and Nut, husband of his sister, Auset, and father of Heru. Set, and Nebt-het are his siblings. He is depicted in numerous forms, but most commonly as a human form with black or green skin (representing death) or as a mummy. He wears a crown and holds a crook and flail criss-crossed against his chest. Originally, Ausar was the Sun god. Later, he was murdered by Set and crowned king of the Underworld/afterlife, and as god of Judgment.

---

1 Geraldine Pinch, *Magic in Ancient Egypt* (Austin, TX: University of Texas Press, 1995), p. 39.

Magicians used decrees issued by Ausar to cure fevers or prolong life span. He assisted in agricultural rituals. Magicians threatened his mummy with destruction to achieve magical goals. The djed pillar amulet is his backbone. He and Auset were depicted in love spells in which the magician targeted a couple and worked to have them develop love and devotion.

Auset (Isis): Wife of Ausar and mother of Heru. She is known as the Great Goddess-mother of the gods, Divine Mother, the Mistress of Charms or Enchantments. She is a great magician, depicted as a woman with a crown that has the horns of a cow (which is sacred to her) surrounding a Sun disk. Her crown is also adorned with feathers and plumes. The scorpion goddess, Serqet, is one of her forms. Auset's power is revered and used in nearly every type of Egyptian magic.

Bat: Goddess who personifies the sistrum of Het-heru.

Edjo: A predynastic cobra goddess with whom Auset left Heru when she went to track down the body of Ausar, who had been murdered by Set. Edjo is a form of the Eye of Ra, the solar eye. She is depicted as a woman and as a cobra, and was placed on the crowns of gods, pharaohs, and other royalty as a symbol of protection who would spit fire at enemies. She also indicated dominion over the land. In magic, she is used as a protective symbol and amulet.

Hedjhotep: A god of weaving and amulets that is invoked to assist in magical work of knots and making amulets.

Heka: A god of magic and the soul of the Sun god. Every magical act is a creative process, and he is the energy that makes creation possible. Heka is depicted in human form, with signs written above his head to form his name. He symbolizes magic, and his power is helpful in all magical deeds.

Heru (Horus): Son of Ausar and Auset. He battles as daylight and order against Set, the night and chaos. Heru is a sky god and a form of the Sun god. Both aspects are symbolized by a falcon. His left eye (the Eye of Heru), is of the Moon, and his right eye (the Eye of Ra) is of the Sun. Separated, or together, the eyes are powerful amulets of protection and empowerment.

Heru is invoked for healing magic and his power is used to charge many temporary and permanent amulets. In written magic, magicians created scripts that prompted shape-shifting into the form of Heru to battle enemies and to meet other needs.

Het-Heru (Hathor): Sky goddess, fertility goddess, and goddess of love, beauty, and happiness. Het-heru is also associated with the Eye of Ra. Many goddesses, such as Auset and Sekhmet, evolved from her. She is depicted as a woman wearing a disk and cow horns atop her head. At other times, she is pictured with the head of a lion surmounted by a uraeus. The sistrum, a type of rattle personified by Bat, is a sacred instrument of hers. Fertility rituals, love spells, magic used in childbirth, and amulets are created to capture her power.

Khepera: God of the rising Sun at dawn. He represents a polarity—matter at the threshold of crossing from inertness into life, and the spirit of the dead preparing for rebirth into a new, glorified form of life. He is depicted as a man, with a scarab beetle for a head. Among ancient nations, the scarab was his emblem, because it was believed to be self-generating. Myriad scarabs found in tombs of all ages in Egypt, the Greek islands, cultures of the Mediterranean, Syria, Phoenicia, and elsewhere were created with this notion in mind. His most popular use in magic is the scarab amulet, which symbolizes becoming and the process of creation.

Maat: Daughter of Ra and the personification of the divine order of things, truth, and justice. Maat also represents the cycles of time, planets, stars, and seasons. She is depicted as a woman wearing an ostrich plume on her head, which is the hieroglyphic symbol for her name and the noun for "truth." Maat represents social and religious order between humanity and the deities, humanity and the dead, and between humans. All must strive to uphold *maat*: truth, justice, and divine order.

Magic and religious rituals were used to preserve the balance and vitality of the universe and its inhabitants. Magic was used as a way of upholding maat. In the papyrus, *The Book of the Heavenly Cow*, a spell instructs the magician to paint a figure of the goddess Maat on his tongue to assure that he spoke the truth. Thus, whatever his words stated would become reality. Maat can be employed in a variety of spells. She can be depicted in figures, pictures, carved onto amulets, or portrayed in statues.

Mut: Mother goddess-wife of the god, Amun. She is symbolic of maternal love and protection and was possibly the original deity at Thebes. On surviving monuments, she is shown in human form, but is thought to have been worshiped in predynastic times in the form of a griffin-vulture. Her name is written using the hieroglyph for "vulture."

Nebt-het (Nephthys): Daughter of the primordial sky goddess, Nut, and the Earth god, Seb. Ausar, Auset, and Set are her siblings.

Nebt-het helped Auset search for Ausar's murdered body. She is among the goddesses of spinning and weaving who produced linen cord for amulets, and is present at births to seal the birthing room with protection and to assist in the childbearing. She is a protector of, and an aid to, women. She is summoned in some health-related spells.

Nekhbet: A protectress and goddess worshiped in the form of a vulture. At times, she was depicted as a cobra. In early Egypt, Nekhbet protected the Pharaoh of Upper Egypt. When the two halves of Egypt were united by Menes, he adopted Nekhbet and Edjo, and identified himself with both deities.

Nekhbet graced the broad collars and pectorals worn against the chest of Pharaohs, as well as other royal jewelry. Queens wore her upon their headdresses. On jewelry, her talons hold a *shen* sign, 𓍶, which depicts the course of the Sun and means "to encircle." Nekhbet protected universally. By the magic of amulets, she protected the Pharaoh, all royalty, births, and women. Sometimes she was equated with Het-heru.

Neith: A powerful creator goddess. She was employed in antivenom and defensive spells inscribed on the statues of deities, Pharaohs, royal officials, and priests. Temples devoted to her often included renowned physicians. Neith ties the magical knots of cords and helps to make amulets of health.

Ptah: One of the oldest gods of Egypt. He is identified with the initial land that came forth from primeval water. He created other deities by his will and the "thoughts of his heart and the words of his mouth." The power of his creative utterance in summoning deities and humanity into existence was sought by ancient magicians. He is also the husband of Sekhmet.

Ptah is usually depicted as a human shrouded like a mummy. He wears a wedge-shaped beard. Upon his shoulders he wears a broad collar with the menat hanging at the base of his neck. His head is shaven, as a priest, and he wears a crown of the Sun disk flanked by two feathers. He is often pictured standing upon a plinth shaped base:

which is the hieroglyph for "maat." His hands, which project from the mummy wrappings, hold the *waas*-scepter, meaning dominion, and the *djed*, meaning stability. The crook, flail, and ankh are also associated with him.

Although a creator god, he is also credited with the invention of crafts and craftsmen. He was summoned in magic relating to the crafts, trades, and occasionally, medicine.

Ra: A solar god who is the visible emblem of divine power. Originally, he was both male and female, allowing him to generate himself and create new life. He fathered Shu, the air god, and Tefnut, the moisture goddess. When they became lost in the darkness of the early world, he sent out his solar eye to find them, lighting up the darkness like the Sun.

Ra is usually depicted in human form, and sometimes with the head of a hawk. He wears the Sun disk upon his head, surmounted by a cobra. Often he holds a scepter and an ankh. Ra appointed Sekhmet as the goddess of his solar eye. She is often invoked in magic, such as love spells, to deliver Ra's power through the solar eye. The solar energy of the Eye of Ra was invoked in magic rituals for protection. The solar eye is known to have had awesome power, especially in defensive magic. Some of Ra's priests were known to have been great seers. Ra's enemies were often mentioned in written magic, or through pictures, to represent enemies to be defeated in spells.

Ra was employed in medicine spells as well. In the *Papyrus Westcar*, Ra sends five goddesses, disguised as dancers, to assist a woman giving birth to triplets. In other papyri, Ra sends his servant and other aids to women giving birth, or to the sick.

Renenutet (Renenet): Goddess of fertility, harvest, fate, fortune, and plenty. She is often mentioned with the god of destiny and fate, Shay. Renenutet is personified as a cobra.

Seb (Geb): Earth god. The children of Ra, Shu and Tefnut, were lovers. They produced Seb and his sister Nut, the sky goddess. From the union of Seb and Nut, Ausar, Haroeris (a form of Heru), Set, Auset, and Nebt-het were born.

Seb is depicted as a man carrying a goose, as a goose-headed man, or a goose. At other times, he is pictured as a man recumbent on the Earth beneath a sky depicted in the shape of a woman, Nut. Seb was benevolently disposed to the world and humanity. He was a fertility god for animals and was invoked in healing spells to cure fevers and colds.

Sekhmet: Daughter of Ra who is the lion-headed goddess of war and strife. As the darker side of her sister, Het-heru, she can take the form of the solar eye. She is the wife of Ptah and is usually depicted as a woman with the head of a lion. She helped to slaughter the enemies of deities, Pharaohs, and humanity, but was also a mistress of healing. The Egyptians believed certain illnesses were caused by evil spirits and thought it best to fight them by invocation of the goddess of war. Sekhmet's ancient priests became known as doctors for their great works of healing and she was employed mostly for defensive and healing magic.

Serqet: Scorpion goddess who assisted at the birth of gods and Pharaohs. Scorpions represented the forces of chaos and dangerous creatures in daily life. The Egyptians flattered Serqet to fend off chaos, the daily threat of scorpions, and cure the effects of scorpion stings. She is depicted as a woman with a scorpion on her head. Amulets and spells captured the power of Serqet and directed it to protection and healing. She is known to have graced the amulets of women and children in particular, offering them her protection.

Set: One of the oldest Egyptian gods, son of Nut and Geb, and husband of his sister, Nebt-het. He helped defeat the enemies of Ra, but later murdered his brother, Ausar, out of jealousy. Then, Heru, the son of Ausar, decided to avenge his father by fighting Set. Set wounded the Eye of Heru, which Tehuti restored.

Set was not always considered a lord of chaos. In early Egypt, he was adored as a royal god who defeated enemies. One theory is that Set, depicted with red-colored skin, became associated with the red desert, which was not fertile. He became known as "the evil day on which nothing can be conceived or born." Thereafter, he was an angry, lustful, and jealous god.

The animal who represents Set is a subject widely debated among Egyptologists. A species of dog, a giraffe, a saluki, and a warthog are among the guesses. He has the body of a greyhound, an elongated and descending muzzle, and erect ears with flattened tips. His eyes are almond-shaped, and a long, forked tail stands upright from his body. Usually, Set is pictured as a masculine, human man with a head as described above.

Set was invoked in defensive magic, healing spells, and to protect magicians from evoked, hostile entities. He may have been included in spells regarding sex, as he was known to have an insatiable lust. For the Egyptians, who believed in fighting like with like, there is no one better for fighting evil than Set.

Shai (Shay): The personification of the lifespan and destiny who decreed the fate of individuals. He had two wives, both goddesses of fate: Renenutet and Meskhenet. He is often depicted as a human man with hieroglyphs that form his name:

Shu: The air god who filled the cosmos with the breath of life. He is the son of Ra and twin brother-husband of Tefnut. With Tefnut, he fathered Nut and Seb. Shu is a messenger of Ra. He sometimes exchanges roles with Heka as a god of magic. Shu's power is invoked in healing spells and various types of magic. He may have been summoned as a messenger to, or from, the deities.

Souchos: The god of the lamp. He is believed to reside in the lamp oil during divination, and he appears as a shadow.

Tefnut: The moisture goddess, daughter of Ra, and twin sister-wife of Shu. She is depicted as a woman with the head of a lioness surmounted by a disk, or as a cobra. Her presence is not frequent in magic, but she was summoned in healing spells.

Tehuti (Thoth): God of divine intelligence, the Moon, writing, speaking, right and truth, and calculating time. He is scribe to the gods, messenger of the gods, and god of human scribes. He usually appears as a man with the head of an ibis. Sometimes his head is adorned with a crescent Moon, lying on its back with points up, a Sun disk atop the Moon, and a plume projecting from the center. He holds a reed pen in his left hand, and an ink palette or papyrus roll in his right.

Tehuti restored Heru's lunar eye when it was destroyed by Set. He is the protector and guardian of both the lunar and solar eyes. Having invented hieroglyphic script, he wrote the forty-two books of law, religious doctrine, and magic. Tehuti created the palette, ink jars, and other implements used by scribes. Above all, Tehuti is a master magician. Magicians of ten shape-shifted into Tehuti to work magic. His power was invoked for numerous magical spells, often by making a wax baboon. Ibis and baboon amulets represent him and are charged with his power. The officiants in medical spells are often identified with Tehuti, and his power is used in healing.

Weret-heka: Goddess of magic, and the power inborn in the royal crowns. She is usually shown in cobra form. The serpent-shaped magical rods employed by magicians likely represented her. Her form and name also appear on the apotropaic wands of magicians. Snake amulets were made to harness her power for various magical uses.

Glossary of Terms

amulet: Any object charged with recited words of power, or written magic, that is worn or carried. Amulets can be temporary or permanent.

amuletic decree: Written magic scripts of the second and first millennium B.C. issued by deities to protect, empower, or otherwise serve with special powers.

apotropaic wand: Curved wand, resembling a throwstick or boomerang, used by magicians in ceremony.

bowl: Typical round dish used to hold water or oil for scrying.

chrysolite: Green or yellow silicate of magnesium and iron used as a semi-precious stone, as described in chapter 3.

dynasty: Division of Egyptian history invented by the scholar-priest Manetho in the third century B.C. The divisions are situated by families of Pharaohs.

Egyptian Book of the Dead: Contemporary name for the *Book of Going Forth by Day*. An illustrated series of funerary spells, written on papyrus, to help the dead travel to, through, and exist in the afterlife.

eye-paint: Ointment placed in the eyes during divination so that deities, evoked beings, and spirits may be seen. It is usually made from an herb or a mixture of plants and animal parts.

faience: Quartz sand melted in a container with pure soda, allowed to cool, and solidified into a glaze. Copper filings were added at the time of heating to make the colors turquoise and green.

Graeco-Egyptian magical papyri: Series of spells written in the Egyptian demotic script, or in Greek, of the first and fifth centuries A.D.

heka: Magical power.

hieroglyphs: Egyptian picture-writing. The word is formed of two Greek words: *hieros* (sacred) and *glypho* (sculptures).

House of Life: Center within a temple that functioned as a school and library.

lamp: Oil lamp used in divination, usually for fire scrying. Egyptian divination lamps were strictly white in color. Many were made from alabaster.

Lower Egypt: Northern Egypt.

maat: A concept of divine order, truth, and justice that the Egyptians strove to maintain. Represented by the goddess Maat.

natron: Arabic word defining a mineral compound of hydrous sodium-carbonate which is usually found in crystalline form with other salts. Used in embalming with other salts, spices, and resins, like myrrh. It is heated to make a liquid to be mixed with honey.

nome: A Greek word that describes an administrative province of Egypt.

obelisk: Shaft of stone with a pointed top. Large obelisks built in Egypt served as talismans.

pantheistic deity: Powers and forms of several deities combined into one divine vehicle, often used in defensive magic.

papyrus: Tall water plant of the sedge family that grew abundantly in delta marshes and other areas of Egypt. The pith of this plant was used for making writing sheets. It was also used for making sandals, ropes, and baskets.

predynastic: The prehistoric period in Egypt, before 3100 B.C.

sau: Person, spell, or amulet that created magical protection.

scrying: Art of divination by gazing and concentrating upon an object, natural or man-made, and obtaining prophetic visions through trance. The Egyptians used fire, water, oil, the Sun, the Moon, and constellations for scrying.

Seven Arrows of Sekhmet: Seven arrows used in magic that bring misfortune and negative results, such as illness. Used to inflict misfortune on enemies.

Seven Het-herus: A sevenfold form of the goddess Het-heru that is a positive force in magic. They were invoked in love spells. They decreed the fate of newborns.

spirit-gathering: Term used for preparing the self , location, and materials for divination.

Upper Egypt: Southern Egypt.

vessel: Any type of container, such as a vase or bowl, used for water or oil scrying.

Wedjat: The Egyptian name of the Eye of Heru; lunar eye.

Egyptian Resources

The following are commercial mail-order sources where you can purchase many of the Egyptian magical tools and supplies discussed herein.

Museum Classics
447 Graceland Dr.
Laguna Beach, CA 92651
(800) 681-MUSE
Fax: (949) 497-5114
E-mail: muse@fea.net

This company offers replicas of Egyptian statues found in the Cairo Museum.

Helen McCrea
150 Inyo Ct.
San Bruno, CA 94066
(650) 873-8793
Fax: (650) 873-9493

She offers a wide range of items; Egyptian replica statues, champagne glasses, papyrus sheets, hand-painted papyrus pictures, stationary, jewelry, and more. Her prices are reasonable and shipping is fast.

Saqqara Technology
47 Sandfield Rd.
Oxford OX3 7RW, England
Telephone/Fax: +44-1865-744505
E-mail: SaqqaraT@aol.com or Saqqara@compuserve.com

This company sells an InScribe Egyptian word processing software program which allows you to enter text by sign menus or transliteration. You can write all of your magical script in hieroglyphs on your computer. This software is for Windows.

Nile Imports Suite N-123
3100 Meridian Parke Drive
Greenwood, IN 46142
(800) 995-6453
Fax: (317) 889-7994

Fine Egyptian handicrafts, such as personalized cartouche jewelry, perfume bottles, mouski glass, amulets, and more.

Museum of Fine Arts, Boston
Catalog Sales Department
P.O. Box 244
Boston, MA 02322-0244

Their catalog offers amulets and other jewelry, games, mummy masks, notepads, puzzles, and items for magic or fun.

New Age Suppliers

The following list of mail-order companies supplies quality incense, natural inks, oils, stones, herbs, jewelry, and other ritual tools for your practice.

AzureGreen
48 Chester Rd.
P.O. Box 48
Middlefield, MA 01243-0048
(413) 623-2155
Fax: (413) 623-2156
E-mail: Abyssdist@aol.com website: www.Azuregreen.com

Marlar Worldwide Company
P.O. Box l 7095AE
Minneapolis, MN 55417
Charge for catalog is $2.00

Church Goods Co.,
Dept. NW 801 W. Jackson Blvd.
Chicago, IL 60607
Fax: (312) 332-3012

Bibliography

Allen, Thomas George. *The Egyptian Book of the Dead or Going Forth By Day*. Studies in Ancient Oriental Civilization, The Oriental Institute of the University of Chicago, No. 37. Chicago, IL: University of Chicago Press, 1960.

Bonner, Campbell. *Studies in Magical Amulets Chiefly Graeco-Egyptian.* Ann Arbor, MI: Harvard Theological Review 39 (1946): 25-55, 1950.

Brier, Bob. *Ancient Egyptian Magic.* New York: William Morrow and Co., Inc. Quill Books, 1981.

Budge, E. A. Wallis. *The Egyptian Book of the Dead.* New York: Dover, 1967.

——. *Egyptian Magic.* New York: Dover, 1971.

Casson, Lionel. *Treasures of the World Series: The Pharaohs.* Chicago, IL: Stonehenge Press, 1981.

Clark, R. T. Rundle. *Myth and Symbol in Ancient Egypt*. London: Thames and Hudson, 1959, reprinted 1978.

Edwards, I. E. S. *Oracular Amuletic Decrees of the Late New Kingdom*, 2 vols. Hieratic Papyri in the British Museum, 4th series. London: Published by Trustees of the British Museum, 1960.

Faulkner, R. O. *The Ancient Egyptian Coffin Texts*, 3 vols. Reprint. Warminster, England: Aris and Phillips, 1978.

——. *The Ancient Egyptian Pyramid Texts*, Reprint. London: Oxford University Press, 1969.

Frankfort, Henri. *Ancient Egyptian Religion*. New York: Harper Torchbooks, 1961.

Ghalioungui, Paul. *Medicine and Magic in Ancient Egypt.* Amsterdam: B.M. Israel, 1973.

Griffith, F. L., and Herbert Thompson, eds., *The Leyden Papyrus: An Egyptian Magical Book.* New York: Dover, 1974

Harris, J. R., ed. *The Legacy of Ancient Egypt.* Oxford: Oxford University Press, 1971.

Knight, Gareth. *Magic and the Western Mind.* St. Paul, MN: Llewellyn, 1991.

K*M*T*, *A Modern Journal of Ancient Egypt,* 3 Volumes: vol. 6, No. 1 Spring 1995; vol. 6, No. 2 Summer 1995; and vol. 6, No. 4 Winter 1995—1996.

Jung, Carl G. *The Collected Works of C. G. Jung,* vol. 6 *Psychological Types,* 2nd ed. Princeton, NJ: Princeton University Press; London: Routledge & Kegan Paul, 1971.

de Meynard, B., and P. de Courteille, eds. *Les Prairies d'Or.* Paris, 1863.

Newsweek/Mondadori. *Great Museums of the World: Egyptian Museum Cairo.* New York: Newsweek, Inc. and Arnoldo Mondadori Editore, 1977.

Pinch, Geraldine. *Magic in Ancient Egypt.* Austin, TIC: University of Texas Press, 1995.

Sauneron, Serge. *The Priests of Ancient Egypt.* New York: Grove Press, 1960.

Time-Life Books, Editors. *TimeFrame 3000-1500 BC: The Age of God-Kings.* Alexandria, VA: Time-Life Books, Inc., 1987.

Watterson, Barbara. *Gods of Ancient Egypt.* New York: Facts on File, 1985.

Index

Eleanor Harris has studied and practiced Egyptian divination and magic for more than nine years. She inherited interest in Egyptian religion and magic from her father. For the past several years, Eleanor has been active in a contemporary Egyptian "House of Life," which is dedicated to teaching and practicing traditional Egyptian magic. She earned her title *Qematet en Tehuti*, "Priestess of Thoth," by authoring literary works, lecturing, and providing workshops for interested students. Her other books are *The Crafting and Use of Ritual Tools*, and *Pet Loss: A Spiritual Guide* both published by Llewellyn.

To Our Readers

Weiser Books, an imprint of Red Wheel/Weiser, publishes books across the entire spectrum of occult, esoteric, speculative, and New Age subjects. Our mission is to publish quality books that will make a difference in people's lives without advocating any one particular path or field of study. We value the integrity, originality, and depth of knowledge of our authors.

Our readers are our most important resource, and we appreciate your input, suggestions, and ideas about what you would like to see published.

Visit our website at *www.redwheelweiser.com* to learn about our upcoming books and free downloads, and be sure to go to *www.redwheelweiser.com/newsletter/* to sign up for newsletters and exclusive offers.

You can also contact us at info@rwwbooks.com or at

Red Wheel/Weiser, LLC

65 Parker Street, Suite 7

Newburyport, MA 01950